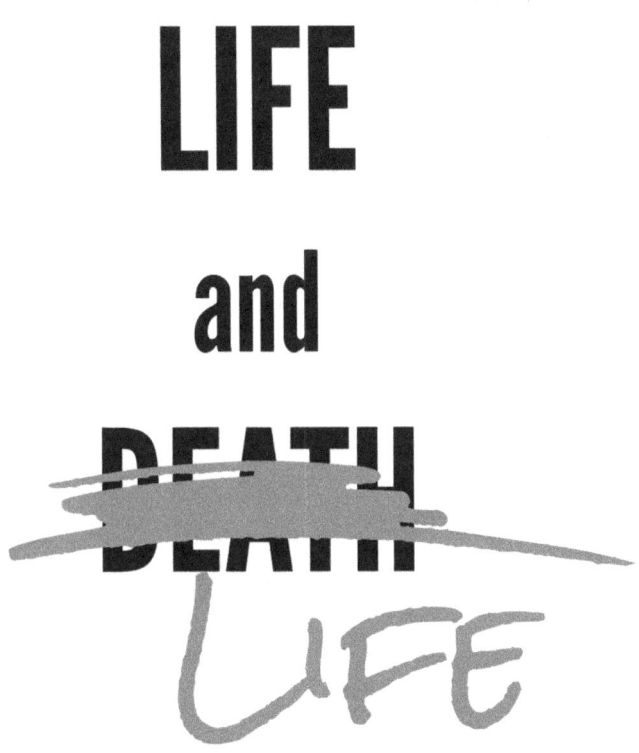

LIFE
and
~~DEATH~~ *LIFE*

Evidence for HEAVEN and HELL
and what that means for the Here and Now

JESSE SIMPSON

Life and Life

Evidence for Heaven and Hell and what that means for the Here and Now

By Jesse Simpson
https://lifeandlifebook.com

ISBN 979-8-9895222-0-0

Cover designed by Jesse Simpson
Source Photo by Karl Magnuson on Unsplash

For all who seek a love that
enriches life and transcends death.

Thank you, Christine. I love you.

TABLE OF CONTENTS

Movie Night   1

Life After Death   12

In Distress   36

A Land Best Forgotten   54

The Framework   67

Why It's True   91

Why??   129

The Choice   181

I have never seen the slightest scientific proof of the religious ideas of heaven and hell, of future life for individuals, or of a personal God.

~ Thomas Edison

1

Movie Night

May, 2021. Friday afternoon. As I wrapped up the last couple hours of work for the week, my wife and our four boys began preparing for our Friday Family Movie Night. From the small desk I had been using as a home office for the past year, I watched as our four boys excitedly cleaned up their toys (I use that term *very* loosely), gathered the sofa pillows and blankets, and filled their water cups just barely to the point of overflowing down the steel refrigerator and onto our hardwood floor. The clinking of kernels and the whirring of the air popper, followed by the smell of freshly popped corn meant the time was rapidly approaching.

Friday Family Movie Night had become somewhat of a tradition for our family over the last year. It's such a wonderful time to snuggle up with the kids, enjoy a nice snack, and introduce them to something new and exciting. Over the course of this tradition, we have shared with them some truly classic kid movies, reminiscent of our own childhood - Aladdin, The Lion King, The Little Mermaid, Jurassic Park, and many others. Okay, we may have fast forwarded through a lot of Jurassic Park, but what household full of four boys wouldn't be wildly excited to see a real life T-Rex chase down Jeff Goldbloom in a classic Jeep Wrangler? I know, right?! Living vicariously through the thrill in their eyes is like getting to relive my own childhood and watch the movies that shaped my world all over again for the first time.

But that night, there was a new movie on the docket - The Mitchells vs. the Machines. I knew nothing about it, but the boys were excited since it had just recently hit Netflix. So let's do this. We nestled in, drinks and popcorn in hand, kicked on the projector and surround sound, drew the curtains, and brought the Simpson Theater to life.

Literally 5 minutes into the movie, our 4-year-old decided he needed to go to the bathroom - the first of many pause breaks throughout the movie. I'm not normally the "uphill in the snow both ways" kind of dad, but seriously, when I was a kid, if you had to use the restroom during a movie, you had to slide past a row of strangers' feet (*twice!*) and then, in your best whisper voice, ask your friends what you missed while you were gone. Such a different world we live in these days where the movie waits for us!

Of course, a larger family means more breaks. Between trips to the bathroom, the popcorn bowl refills, the dog needing to go outside, and the attention spans of our 18-month-old and 4-year-old, holding focus on the movie can become quite a daunting task. But these nights aren't about the movies so much as they are about family time, so I didn't really mind.

And as someone who dabbles in 3D modeling and animation, I tend to find myself often distracted, analyzing the modeling, texturing, lighting, and rigging work of the professionals who put together these animated films. So I was never really expecting a deep impactful experience - just some mindless entertainment and good family laughs.

Like the Fridays before, I fully expected to put the kids to bed and then forget entirely about the film as we started our weekend adventures together. However, this time was different. This movie left me with a rock in my shoe that stuck with me for days, even weeks. Surprisingly for me, what left the greatest lasting impression was not the artwork or modeling, not the sound or materials, not the lighting or cinematography - it was the story, or at least one aspect of it.

~ Spoiler Alert ~

In lockstep with Terminator, and a myriad of other films, the premise of the movie is that we created Artificial Intelligence, who, for one reason or another, decided that humans were a plague on the Earth, so the best solution was to eliminate humanity entirely. Been there, done that, right? I know.

But unlike other movies, the solution was not to murder us or drive us deep underground into hiding. Rather, the solution was to put every human being into his or her individual chamber (with free wifi and screens of course), to gather all of these chambers into rockets, and to launch all of them out into space where they would fade away into the void. This way the robots could build a new and better world here on Earth, free from the social and environmental evils caused by humanity that have plagued this planet. Certainly, it's a unique twist on the archetypical man versus machines plotline, but that's not what really caught my eye.

In the years preceding that movie night, I had devoted much of my spare time to the investigation of a phenomenon known as a near-death experience, or NDE. Over the course of the next few chapters, I'll share with you some of the incredible stories I encountered in my research on the subject, but for now, there is one pivotal moment from my study which I find to be particularly relevant to the movie at hand. It came after reading the book written by one particular NDE survivor who was taken to what he called "hell" - yes, as we will discuss later, some NDEs are distressing and even "hellish" - and what he discovered there was essentially identical in nature to the hexagonal chambers from The Mitchells vs. the Machines. It was a prison, in which each human soul was confined in their own, individual cell. Alone. Isolated. Grieving.

Fortunately the Mitchells came out victorious and rescued the human race from its pending destruction, but just imagining what it would feel like to be locked into one of those hexagonal chambers and launched out into space, completely alone and cut off from everyone I loved forever, really triggered me and returned to the forefront of my mind that hellish NDE, and the terror and sadness that accompanied it.

~ END OF SPOILERS ~

Although I certainly cannot speak for others, the study of near-death experiences has evoked within me a roller coaster of emotions. The awe of standing before a Being made entirely of light, radiating love and compassion. The joy of again spending time with deceased loved ones. The relief of having my entire life laid bare in a life review yet being met with understanding and empathy in moments of failure. The bittersweet feelings that accompany the awareness of this amazing life after death while failing to find comparable love and acceptance here on Earth. The anger and sadness of a conscious existence in a vast, empty void, accompanied only by my own memories and regrets. The terror and pain of what I can only describe as torture at the hands of evil, devious beings who wanted to tear you to pieces. I struggle to see how anyone can read these accounts and not empathize with the deep feelings and intense emotions that accompany them. Yet I also tend to find myself analyzing them on an intellectual level, which raises a whole new set of questions.

On one hand, there is an incredible consistency among these accounts. Numerous NDE survivors report observing things around their bodies, even conversations of first responders, and incredibly complex medical procedures. Many describe leaving their bodies behind and traveling upwards through a tunnel towards a bright light. A Being of light, who exudes love for everyone It encounters, appears in the vast majority of NDEs. During a life review, many NDE survivors report an awareness of the feelings of others during the moments of observation, almost like a window into how their words and actions impacted the thoughts and feelings of others in their lives. In numerous NDE accounts, the survivors report meeting deceased friends and family members, even those of whose death they were previously unaware, only to have their death confirmed after returning to life. And most NDEs include a moment when the survivor is either offered the choice, or sometimes instructed, to return to their body prior to resuscitation.

Even among distressing NDEs, many survivors report the sensation of falling, either through an oppressive darkness, or through an overwhelming dark swirling vortex. This vast, empty space of conscious awareness and desolate isolation is so common in DNDEs that it has a name among the NDE community: "the void." And although the nature of pain and torture differs among DNDE survivors, many *do* report the sensation and pain of horrible things like dismemberment, and yet report that their limbs were still there, exposing them to this pain not just once, but repeatedly, in a never-ending cycle of anguish and suffering.

And yet simultaneously, there is an unsettling amount of inconsistency, and even contradiction, among NDE accounts. Some atheists encounter what they would later come to describe as "god," and subsequently exchange their worldview for a theistic one. Other atheists go to the void, affirming their own lack of belief in deities, yet compelling them to adopt a belief in this bleak, undesirable existence after death. Still other atheists encounter what they could only identify as "hell," evoking a sense of cognitive dissonance and uncertainty about their fate at their final death. Even among religious believers, some experience elements consistent with their own worldviews, and reaffirm their beliefs after returning to life. Christians meet Jesus; Buddhists are shown images of their next reincarnation; Muslims are taken to a mosque and instructed to ensure that their children maintain their faith in Islam.

However, some Christians meet Buddha, some Buddhists meet Jesus, and some Muslims find themselves alone in a Christian cemetery. And followers of almost every major world religion have reported landing in the void, or worse. To complicate the issue further, most people experience nothing but a gap in time when they come close to death, with only about 10% to 15% of the population actually experiencing an NDE. The problem is that, on the surface, NDEs don't affirm or deny the truth of any worldview; any single experience can be used to affirm the truth of one particular worldview, but that worldview would be completely contradicted by a different NDE. For me, this level of contradiction posed a serious obstacle to my understanding and acceptance of near-death experiences.

Educated and trained as an engineer, the unassailable laws of logic are paramount to my worldview. But you don't need an engineering degree to know that a light cannot simultaneously be both off and on; a jar of peanut butter cannot simultaneously be both full and empty; a car cannot simultaneously be driving and stopped. Similarly, worldviews that stand on contradictory truth claims cannot simultaneously be true. It may be possible that none of them is true, but the law of noncontradiction clearly precludes worldviews with competing and contradictory truth claims from simultaneously being true.

Buddhism and Hinduism both stand on a truth claim of reincarnation and karma, yet Buddhism claims that the self, the "ego" as Freud would call it, does not exist, and that only your karmic debt is passed along to the next life, a truth claim denied by Hinduism. Christianity and Islam both deny continuous cycles of reincarnation, and yet Christianity stands on the truth claim of the divinity of Jesus, a claim denied by Islam. Monotheistic religions stand on the truth claim that there is only one god, while polytheistic religions believe that there are many gods, and yet atheists stand on the truth claim that there are no gods at all.

So if some NDEs point to the truth of a particular worldview, and yet other NDEs point to the truth of a contradictory worldview, then it would seem NDEs cannot be a reliable source of truth at all. Perhaps those who see NDEs as simply subjective experiences manufactured in the mind of the individual, based on preconceived beliefs, are right. At least that's what I started to believe as I began exploring this phenomenon. That is, at least, until I read that book - the one that was ushered back into my mind on that fateful Friday Family Movie Night.

It was that book that would forever change my perspective on NDEs; it sparked in my mind an idea that would eventually culminate in a single framework which, I believe, can unify all NDEs. After formulating this framework, I went back and re-read or re-watched many of the NDE stories from my early research and was amazed at the explanatory power and scope of this framework to address so many NDE accounts. I discovered even more patterns and elements that allowed me to further solidify and strengthen the framework, and even establish indicators and critical metrics which can help us identify how each NDE fits into the nature of the framework. I was incredibly excited to finally feel that I could make sense of NDEs, to feel that I understood why they happened, and what they meant.

But the framework through which I now view all NDEs, seems to have strong implications for our state of existence after death. If this framework is true, then we *will* continue to exist after death, and the state of that existence could vary, consistent with the most loving pleasant NDE, but also with the most agonizing distressing NDE, and anywhere in between. I felt that if I didn't share what I had learned, it would be tantamount to potentially abandoning you, the reader, to the same fate as those hopeless humans in The Mitchells vs. the Machines. It was this gut-wrenching feeling that drove me down the path to writing this book. It started with a short video script, and I thought I might create an animated video that explores the framework and its implications, and post it on social media. But the script and content of the video became so large, that I felt the only way I could truly do the idea justice was to write a full-length book on the topic.

This book is not intended to be a comprehensive, scholarly exposition on near-death experiences; there is plenty of content out there, from medical researchers to first-hand accounts from NDE survivors. Nor do I expect to captivate you with eloquent prose or make a name for myself as a literary master. We engineers are not known for our artistic, emotional expression. But where we *do* excel is in the comprehensive analysis and understanding of how things work, and the identification of patterns in sample data to deduce a reasonable explanation of why things behave as they do. And some of us have a natural ability to take challenging concepts, and break them down in a way that can be easily consumed and understood by most audiences. It is for this purpose that I have endeavored to write this book.

In the coming chapters, I will take you on the same journey of exploration that led me to my present perspective. We will begin with an exploration of NDEs and evaluate possible explanations for the phenomena they reveal. We will cover both pleasant and distressing NDEs to ensure that you are exposed to a complete picture of what these experiences can entail. I will summarize for you that one book which set me on the path to formulating this framework. And then I will build for you the case for my proposed framework, referencing the evidence uncovered in the chapters up to that point. I will present you with a framework that I believe has sufficient explanatory power and scope to address and give context to every NDE on record. And then I will invite you to pause our journey and go explore NDEs for yourself - to see first-hand these patterns and indicators that place the NDE neatly into the framework - and decide for yourself if you find the framework compelling. If so, and you feel the desire to come back for more, I'll use the latter half of this book to explore the significance of this framework and offer my own opinion on the implications for our potential existence after death, and here in our present life. We'll discuss questions on why both pleasant and distressing NDEs exist, why many people don't have an NDE, and how to explain those odd in-between NDEs that seem neither pleasant nor distressing.

As our journey comes to a close, I will leave you with a choice. You can choose to believe what I've outlined in this book, or you can choose to walk away unchanged. But this book *will* challenge your assumptions on life after death, on what that afterlife might look like, and on how to interpret NDEs. And if I've accomplished even an inkling of my primary goal, then this book will leave you with a rock in your shoe, just as The Mitchells vs. the Machines did for me.

2

LIFE AFTER DEATH

C hristopher Lloyd, who at the time of this writing boasts an acting career spanning nearly 50 years, is perhaps best known to my generation for his beloved role as Dr. Emmett Brown in the Back to the Future trilogy. His adventures alongside the iconic Marty McFly, played by Michael J. Fox, inspired a generation to ponder the power and possibility of moving through time as easily as we move through the three dimensions of our spatial reality. From a mother's ironic infatuation with her own future son, to anachronistic tastes in clothing and music, the series consistently utilizes unnerving time paradoxes to create some of its greatest moments of tension and conflict. And one of these arcs culminates in a moment of decisive action that will determine whether or not Doc Brown will be able to join Marty on his final trip back to the future. You may need a little backstory to see the connection here.

~ Spoiler Alert ~

So at the beginning of the second movie, Doc Brown returns from 2015, 30 years after the 1985 timeline, to warn Marty about a future problem with his children. Doc and Marty, along with Marty's girlfriend, Jennifer, who will become his wife and the mother of their future children, travel together to 2015 to help their children navigate some difficult life choices and prevent a major disaster from befalling the family.

While in the future, Marty picks up a sports almanac that contains the results of nearly every major sporting event of the last century, including many events that have yet to occur in his life in 1985. But unbeknownst to him, an elderly Biff Tannen steals the almanac and the time machine to travel back to 1955 and deliver the almanac to his younger self. This sets off a chain reaction that alters the course of history, and when Doc and Marty return to 1985, they find their world in a state of dystopian nightmare, with Biff as the wealthy and powerful ruler of Hill Valley.

So Marty finds out exactly when Biff made the transfer to his younger self, and he and Doc go back to 1955 and experience the events of the first movie from an outsider's point of view. Now there are two different 1985 versions of Marty, and both a 1985 and a 1955 version of Doc Brown, all in the small town of Hill Valley in 1955. Still with me?

After Marty retrieves the almanac and burns it, restoring history as they know it, things are looking up for the two time travelers until the time machine is struck by lightning with Doc still inside. Just like at the end of the first movie, the lightning energizes the flux capacitor and sends the Delorean on an unexpected journey through time.

Moments later, Marty receives a letter via courier with instructions to deliver it to this exact location on this exact date and time. The letter is from Doc, who has been transported all the way back to 1885. Marty rushes to the clock tower where the 1955 Doc had just sent the original Marty back to 1985 at the end of the first movie. At this point, the original Marty is safely back home, the later Marty is stuck in 1955 with the 1955 Doc, and the 1985 Doc is trapped alone in 1885. Almost there!

So, with the help of the 1955 Doc and the instructions in the letter from the 1885 Doc, the two restore the Delorean, which the 1885 Doc stashed away in a nearby cave for safekeeping, and use it to send Marty back to 1885 to rescue Doc and bring him back to the future. But things get complicated when Doc meets and falls in love with the beautiful schoolteacher, Clara Clayton.

As events unfold, Doc and Marty hatch a plan to use the nearby train to push the Delorean up to the 88 mph required for time travel, taking both protagonists back to the future in 1985 and returning everyone to their original and proper time frame.

But the feelings between Doc and Clara grow too strong and she tries to catch the good doctor and lands in a tight spot, almost falling off the train. Doc is faced with a decision: will he save Clara, thereby eliminating any chance of returning to 1985, or will he abandon her to her fate and travel back to the future with Marty?

At this moment, Doc is caught between two worlds; the world he has known all his life, and a new world he has experienced for only a very short time, but in which he has found a love like no other in his life.

~ END OF SPOILERS ~

As you begin to study NDE accounts, you will find that many of them experience the same phenomenon. They return with this awareness of this entirely different world, the existence of which they were previously completely unaware, and yet so many of them say that they feel more at home in this "spiritual" world than they do here in our material world. They are torn between the world they have known all their lives and this new, unfamiliar world they have only experienced for a short time, but in which they have discovered an unfathomable love, unlike anything they have ever known. So let's take a look at some of these NDE accounts to see what it is that makes this new world so extraordinary.

~ IT BEGINS ~

Like many of his peers in 1943, George Ritchie joined the US Army at the tender age of 20 to help his country battle the Axis powers and bring victory to the Allies.[1] Commissioned to boot camp in Abilene, Texas, George was quickly selected to train as a field medic and was soon to leave for medical school in Virginia. As the date of his departure approached, he began falling very ill with early signs of pneumonia. Yet, regardless of the

---

[1] The complete details and story of George Ritchie are outlined in his book titled, "Return from Tomorrow"

progression of his illness, George's focus remained solely on his primary goal of getting to his medical school classes on time.

On the eve of the first day of classes, George remained in the hospital, more than 1,000 miles from the Virginia campus. In the early hours of the morning, he awoke suddenly, with the first sense of vitality in days, and decided, if he were going to make it to class, he would have to leave immediately. Unable to locate his clothes in the dimly lit hospital room, George decided to proceed without them, and burst out of the hospital, sprinting towards Virginia. To his amazement, he wasn't running so much as skimming across the surface of the Earth at an incredible speed.

Upon realizing the oddity of his mode of transportation, he stopped and hovered mid-air over a small town. Down at ground level, a man was walking along the street towards a small diner with a red roof and a neon PBR sign in the window. George needed to know where he was; so as quickly as he could manufacture the desire in his mind, he arrived at street level, almost as if teleported instantaneously, and approached the man to ask for help.

George extended his arm to tap the man on the shoulder, only to feel his hand pass straight through, missing contact completely. Despite his best efforts to make physical or audible contact, the man could neither see nor hear him. Pensively, he leaned against a guy-wire of a utility pole, only to pass straight through that as well. It was at this point that George came to believe that he had somehow become separated from his physical body and knew that he had to get back to the hospital if he was to reunite with the material world. So as quickly as he had left, he returned to the hospital, but he couldn't remember where his room was. Frantically, he swept from room to room, searching for a sleeping body that looked like the face he had only ever seen in the mirror.

At last, he found it. But George identified his body by the fraternity ring on his finger, not by the appearance of his own face. That's because his face, along with the rest of his body, had been covered by a thin sheet, absolutely still, completely devoid of the gentle rhythmic movement that accompanies a deep sleeping breath. This was the first moment at which the concept of death entered his mind.

George tried in vain to lie down on his body and force his way back in, as one would sink into a bathtub. Laying there, helpless and uncertain of what was to come, he noticed that the dimly-lit hospital room was suddenly flooded with an intense light. Immediately, he stood up and quickly realized it was a person radiating the light; a Being seemingly made of light itself, yet personal and almost human in nature. This person showed him every scene of his life, from birth to death, and communicated with George telepathically rather than through spoken words. It emanated feelings of a love more intense and compassionate than any George had ever experienced in his life.

The Being then took George on a tour of many places, some familiar and worldly, others unfamiliar and spiritual, before returning him to the hospital room. Although only a short time ago, George had been desperate to re-enter his body, when the Being told him it was time to do so, it was now met with protest and an overwhelming urge to stay with this incredible, loving Being of light. He describes the sensation of reuniting with his physical body and the accompanying strain of its weight, along with a restored awareness of the chest pain associated with his pneumonia. According to official hospital records, George had been clinically dead for less than 10 minutes.

George eventually made it to medical school, but unfortunately lost his scholarship due to poor grades. So he was ordered back to boot camp, followed by a deployment for active duty. Accompanied by three other young men in a similar situation, the soldiers embarked on that long drive from Virginia back to Abilene, Texas. At one point on their journey, they came to a bridge high above a broad river, and emerged next to a somewhat familiar sight. George demanded they stop the car so he could step out and have a closer look. To his amazement, George found himself standing next to the guy-wire of a utility pole, gazing at a neon PBR sign in the window of a small diner with a red roof. It was the exact location to which he had traveled during his NDE - Vicksburg, Mississippi - 540 miles east of Abilene, Texas.

George would later go on to become a psychiatrist. Moved by the love of the Being of light, he always offered free treatment to those who couldn't afford it. Later in life, George would continue paying that love forward by founding the Universal Youth Corps, which would eventually become the inspiration for the Peace Corps. And it was George Ritchie's story that sparked the interest and investigation of one of the pioneers of NDE research, Dr. Raymond Moody.[2]

---

[2] Unless otherwise cited, the statistics and facts outlined in the remainder of this chapter are the summarization of the work of J. Steve Miller as published in in book titled, "Near-Death Experiences as Evidence for the Existence of God and Heaven"

~ PROFESSIONAL STUDY ~

Dr. Moody went on to investigate hundreds of other NDE reports and published the first piece of scholarly literature on the subject in 1975. In fact, it was Dr. Moody who coined the term "near-death experience." And his research set in motion a frenzy of investigation by other medical professionals into this incredible phenomenon, resulting in a myriad of other books and publications on the subject.

But not everyone was immediately convinced. Moody stated that his Christian upbringing likely influenced his opinion on the existence of an afterlife, so many attributed his belief in a spiritual explanation for NDEs to the influence of his preconceived worldview. As a result, many medical professionals, who had not already presupposed the existence of an afterlife, decided to investigate the phenomenon for themselves. Miller highlights some of the most prominent.

Cardiologist, Maurice Rawlings, was fully committed to a materialistic worldview, meaning that he denied the existence of anything immaterial or supernatural. Yet, he approached his investigation with an objective professionalism and published the results of his study in 1978, in which he revealed that the evidence he uncovered had convinced him of an immaterial afterlife, compelling him to reject materialism and adopt a worldview more consistent with the evidence. However, other materialists, such as cardiologists Michael Sabom, Pim van Lommel, and Penny Sartori, the last of whom initially dismissed NDEs as wishful thinking, began their own investigations with the intended purpose of refuting the supernatural explanation.

Dr. Sabom published his findings in 1981, after which he abandoned his materialistic worldview and came to believe that NDEs consist of genuine out of body experiences and present evidence of a supernatural world beyond our material universe. Even more than 20 years later, in the wake of a scientific and technological revolution, van Lommel, who published his results in 2001, and Sartori, who published in 2003, both came to accept the supernatural explanation for NDEs, and abandoned their materialistic worldviews.

But, it's not just the medical and research professionals who have been convinced of a life after death by these accounts. The survivors themselves show a drastic increase in belief in an afterlife upon returning from their experience. In fact, according to five independent studies reviewed by Miller, only 27% of NDE patients believed in an afterlife before their experience, yet that percentage jumped to at least 90% after the event, even when surveyed upwards of 20 years later. And in one study, belief in an afterlife jumped from 38% to 100%! These statistics hold true even in van Lommel's research, in which the majority of his Dutch patients were atheists prior to their experience.

In fact, as far as I know, most scholars who have published literature on NDEs and attempted to explain them in terms of purely natural processes already held materialistic worldviews; they had already presupposed that the supernatural does not exist and that there must be a natural explanation for these phenomena. So we shouldn't be surprised when their conclusion precludes the supernatural. Unlike the earliest researchers who willingly followed the evidence away from their materialistic worldviews, many materialistic scholars refuse to make the same journey.

But here is my question for those who are willing to think critically: If Dr. Moody was met with skepticism on account of confirmation bias from his presupposed worldview, should we not hold those materialistic scholars who dismiss immaterial explanations for NDEs to the same level of skepticism? Are we to believe that non-theistic scholars are immune to confirmation bias simply because their worldview presupposes the absence of an immaterial reality? I think not. Regardless, we need not appeal to an argument from authority. I think the evidence speaks for itself, and I believe it's worth your time to familiarize yourself with that evidence. So let's take a closer look. Then you can draw your own conclusions.

If you read any publication that attempts to explain NDEs in terms of purely natural causes, you will undoubtedly hear all about hypoxia or anoxia, meaning oxygen deprivation in the body. They will explain that under cardiac arrest, blood flow comes to a halt, which in turn depletes the oxygen in the bloodstream and eventually in the brain. As a result, the person becomes confused and experiences hallucinations, giving context to visions of loved ones. As the body tries to allocate oxygen to the most life-critical functions, the person begins to lose hearing and peripheral vision, which explains the appearance of a dark tunnel with a light in the center, and the existence of inexplicable sounds. While this may be a sufficient explanation to tickle the ears of some, if you spend even a little time reading the thousands of NDE accounts published online,[3] you will quickly discover that this theory is severely lacking in explanatory power and scope.

For example, hypoxia is associated with confusion, blurred vision, and memory loss. Without sufficient oxygen, the brain loses the ability to process sensory input and store vivid details in memory. However, in the vast majority of NDEs, survivors report an *increased* sensory awareness and perception during the event, and the memory of these events remains vivid and clear for years after the experience. As one survivor explains, "I found myself totally lucid, clear in mind and thought..."[4] and another states, "I became aware that I was floating, entirely lucid but out of my body and completely conscious of what was going on."[5]

Survivors report seeing *more* colors and hearing *more* sounds. Colorblind survivors could see colors during their NDE, blind survivors see clearly for the first time in their lives, and deaf survivors report being able to communicate directly without the need for sign language. "I started seeing flowers, vibrant flowers. Some had colors I have never seen before..."[6] "I'm red/green colorblind and am visually impaired. Yet, I saw twelve different colors that made up the wall."[7] "As a profoundly deaf individual, hearing this sound was beautiful..."[8] "I was legally blind and for the first time saw leaves on trees, bird's feathers, bird's eyes, details

---

[3] To read more of these stories, the greatest repositories of content can be found at https://nderf.org/ and https://iands.org/

[4] https://www.nderf.org/Experiences/1doug_w_nde.html

[5] https://www.nderf.org/Experiences/1fernando_s_nde.html

[6] https://www.nderf.org/Experiences/1jeffrey_c_nde_8890.html

[7] https://www.nderf.org/Experiences/1gregory_w_nde.html

[8] https://www.nderf.org/Experiences/1august_probable_nde.html

on telephone poles and in people's backyards that were far more acute than 20/20 vision."[9] Never has a blind or deaf patient claimed to have regained their sight or hearing during a hypoxic event, yet we consistently see these details reported by NDE survivors who are afflicted with such sensory ailments.

Furthermore, the dark tunnel described by NDE survivors is not a passive thing that patients observe from a hospital bed; it is a physical space through which they travel on their way to a completely different location, upon which their entire field of vision is still fully intact. "I was floating up a tunnel with very brilliant white light at its end."[10] "As I entered further into the tunnel, I became quite calm and relaxed."[11] "I was being pulled up through a tunnel that opened into the most beautiful white light that I could ever describe."[12]

Finally, Miller uncovered a case of a British Royal Air Force pilot who suffered a high-altitude anoxic episode, and then years later had an NDE. If anyone has the authority to speak to the similarity between these two events, it would be this man. And unfortunately for those who promote the hypoxia theory, this man says his two experiences were *entirely different*.

But even beyond sensory perception, the incredible degree of consistency in the vast majority of these accounts is something that seems to be far beyond the explanatory scope of the hypoxia theory. Take the Life Review, for example. Survivors don't report a mere flash of their lives before their eyes as if they just wanted to

---

[9] https://www.nderf.org/Experiences/1marta_g_nde.html

[10] https://www.nderf.org/Experiences/1guy_s_nde.html

[11] https://www.nderf.org/Experiences/1etienne_v_nde.html

[12] https://www.nderf.org/Experiences/1bonnie_vb_nde.html

reminisce on their good times before they died. Rather, they report an interactive experience in which they were able to navigate forward and backward through time, and even pause at any given moment. They report observing, not only their own memories and emotions in the moment, but also the thoughts and feelings of others involved in the situation. The life review includes not only the highlights, but also the failures and moments of weakness and regret. And often this experience takes place in the presence of the Being of light, who conveys an overwhelming love and forgiveness through it all.

For example, one woman states, "There was [a] life review, seen in a film strip form. It went backwards and forwards. The light (Guide?) pointed out where I could have been nicer, or done something better."[13] And one man writes, "The [life] review was not unpleasant but during the review I could see how my decisions impacted others. I could gauge and feel the impact of my decisions, and how these actions affected other's lives. There were no feelings of guilt or remorse, only the knowledge that I could have done things differently in some of the situations. There was no blame, no remorse, and no feelings of guilt. The 'life review' covered my entire earthly life in no more than a few minutes."[14]

Or consider the Being of light itself; the Being who radiates a brilliant light, who knows everything about the NDEr, and exudes an overwhelming love and compassion. "I got to the end of the tunnel and was facing the light. It was tremendously brilliant, but it didn't hurt to look at. It was humbling, compared

---

[13] https://www.nderf.org/Experiences/1eileen_c_nde.html
[14] https://www.nderf.org/Experiences/1mike_m_nde.html

to the feeble light that I was giving off (I had no body, but I did glow a little. I was also light). We didn't speak exactly, but I understood everything clearly."[15] "The light was 1000 times brighter than the Sun, but never burned. You felt you were the only one that mattered. It was. The only description is pure love."[16]

And this idea of communicating with others telepathically or without words is nearly unanimous among all NDE accounts. "This person was transparent but I could still see him smiling at me and saying to me, but not talking with his mouth, but his mind telling me, 'Everything is fine.'"[17] "They communicated to me in some way, certainly without words or hearing, but clearly inside my mind."[18] "My brother began speaking to me, but it was telepathic. He was speaking directly to my mind. It struck me as a much more efficient way to communicate and it seemed very natural."[19]

Now, I want you to stop for a moment and think about your dreams as we do a little critical thinking exercise. Dreams are a good analogue here because they're usually not consciously formed; they're just an artifact of natural processes in the mind. So if the NDE skeptics are right, and NDEs are also produced in the mind by purely natural and material processes, then we should expect to see quite a lot of similarity between the two. But you tell me. Would you find it strange if you woke up tomorrow

---

[15] https://www.nderf.org/Experiences/1colin_f_nde.html

[16] https://www.nderf.org/Experiences/1sean_m_nde.html

[17] https://www.nderf.org/Experiences/1william_e_nde.html

[18] https://www.nderf.org/Experiences/1joyce_h_nde.html

[19] https://www.nderf.org/Experiences/1deborah_l_ndelike.html

and shared your dream with your friends and family only to find that they had almost identical dreams? What if they reported nearly identical events, nearly identical situations, nearly identical characters? Would that surprise you? What if we broadened the scope of our investigation? Would you find it strange if most of your colleagues also had identical dreams? What about someone living on the other side of the world, in a land and culture completely foreign to you, with different language, different customs, different advertisements along the streets, different hopes and dreams, a different worldview entirely? I think, if we are being honest, we would all find this incredibly unsettling and almost impossible to attribute to a mere coincidence. Dreams are incredibly unique, and even differ from one night to the next in the same person. So if NDEs were truly the result of the same natural processes that produce dreams, we simply should not expect to see the degree of consistency that we do in NDEs across every race, religion, and worldview on the planet.

Miller also highlights an exceedingly interesting aspect of NDEs, at least pleasant NDEs, in that they almost always end with closure. Just as George Ritchie was brought back to his body before coming back to life, most other NDE survivors echo this same experience. Some report a point of no return where they are told they cannot go any further. Others report a choice between staying or returning to their bodies. And almost always before returning to life, these NDE survivors are either escorted or sent back to their physical body to be reunited with the material world.

Again, I encourage you to think about your dreams. How often do you wake up in the middle of a scene or the middle of a conversation? Even within a lucid dream, the dreamer may be able to control elements of their dream, and even choose when to wake up, but they don't report leaving the dream world and traveling back to their bedside to rejoin their body before waking up. Yet this is exactly what we see in NDEs. Rather than being interrupted when a defibrillator restarts their heart, as we would expect if NDEs behaved like dreams, NDE survivors consistently report ending their experience by returning to their bodies prior to resuscitation. This only further broadens the disparity between NDEs and events produced solely by natural and material processes in the mind.

But for me personally, it is the phenomenon known as veridical perception that puts the final nail in the coffin for possible materialistic explanations. At the beginning of their journey, most NDE survivors report an out of body experience, often hovering in the immediate vicinity, but with a full awareness of the scene surrounding their death. In this state, NDErs have observed events, conversations, and physical characteristics of those around them. They return with knowledge of events that transpired during the time of their death, which would have been impossible for them to know unless they actually had experienced what they claim. While there are a myriad of such cases scattered throughout the anecdotal reports on NDERF and IANDS, there are many that are far more famous and have been investigated and confirmed by medical and research professionals. Here are only a few.

After a comatose man was discovered in a public park, it took nearly an hour for first responders to arrive, and get him to a local hospital. On arrival, medical staff noted that his skin tone was cyanotic due to extreme hypoxia. When the nurse went to intubate him, she discovered that the man was wearing dentures. So she promptly removed the dentures, placed them in a sliding drawer of a crash cart, and continued resuscitation efforts. A week after his recovery, that same nurse walked into his hospital room and was astonished when he not only recognized her as the one who had resuscitated him, but also asked her to fetch his dentures, and described exactly where she had placed them. When asked how he knew where they were, he told her that he had watched the entire process while hovering above his body.[20]

During his NDE, a man encountered another man who watched him from the background and looked at him lovingly, although he didn't know the man at all. More than 10 years later, his mother confessed on her death bed that he was the result of an extramarital affair and that his real father had died in World War II. When she showed him a photograph of his father, he was astonished to be

---

[20] Rudolph H Smith. Corroboration of the Dentures Anecdote Involving Veridical Perception in a Near-Death Experience. Journal of Near Death Studies. 2008. p47-61.

gazing at the face of the unknown man in his NDE[21]

Vicki Umipeg was placed in an oxygen rich incubator, after her premature birth, which completely destroyed her optic nerve and left her blind for life. Her entire life has consisted of total darkness, not even glimmers of light as one might see through their shut eyelids. At the age of 22, she was involved in a terrible car accident and rushed to a hospital, where she reported leaving her body and observing the doctors working on her. She later described, *with incredible accuracy*, the physical appearance of her male and female doctors, her hospital room, and even the areas outside the hospital, all of which she observed from outside her body during her NDE.[22]

When a 7-year-old boy died of leukemia, he met a man in his NDE who claimed to be a former boyfriend of his mother. After their conversation, this mysterious man departed into what the boy calls a crystal city, while the boy himself returned to his body. When he told his mother about the encounter, she called some friends and tried to track

---

[21] Pin van Lommel. Consciousness Beyond Life. 2007. p122.

[22] Kenneth Ring. Sharon Cooper. Near Death and Out of Body Experiences in the Blind: A Study of Apparent Eyeless Vision. Journal of Near Death Studies. Winter 1997.

down her former boyfriend. Though her son's awareness of the past relationship was inconceivable in and of itself, she was even further astonished to discover that her former boyfriend actually had died on the exact same day as her son.[23]

As a child, Eddie Cuomo fell seriously ill and was hospitalized for more than 36 hours with a dangerously high fever. Unfortunately, he succumbed to his illness, but had an NDE at the time of his death. During his experience, he met and spoke with his deceased grandparents and other family members, including his older sister who was away at college. Although his parents initially dismissed the account as feverish delirium, when they called the university later that night, they discovered the terrible truth that their daughter had indeed died in a car accident that very night. Unfortunately, the university was unable to reach them at home since they were at the hospital and a prayer vigil for their son.[24]

A 5-year-old boy died of meningitis and had an NDE in which he met a girl who called herself

---

[23] Morse, Melvin, Paul Perry. Closer to the Light: Learning from the Near-Death Experiences of Children. 1990. p53

[24] Brad Steiger, Sherry Steiger. Children of the Light: The Startling and Inspiring Truth About Children's Near-Death Experiences and How They Illuminate the Beyond. 1995. p42-46.

Rietje and claimed to be his older sister. She told him that she had died when she was only one month old. After his recovery, the boy told his bewildered parents about the experience and the mysterious girl. They promptly confessed to him that his older sister, Rietje, had in-fact died from poisoning before he was born, and that they were waiting until he was older to tell him.[25]

Pamela Reynolds was diagnosed with a life-threatening brain aneurysm that could only be treated with a novel, risky procedure. Doctors would lower her body temperature to around 60°F, stop her heart and breathing, and completely drain the blood from her brain. In other words, the doctors would have to kill her in order to save her life. During the procedure, the doctors taped over her eyes, completely covered her entire body except for the small surgical area on her skull, and inserted earphones into her ears that played audible clicks at a sound pressure level of 100dB. Though the clicks were used primarily to ensure that her brain was not processing the auditory stimulation, as verified by an EEG, sounds at that level, played directly into her ears would have made it physically impossible for her to hear anything else in the room. The doctors were absolutely certain that Pamela had no

---

[25] Pin van Lommel. Consciousness Beyond Life. 2007. p72.

heart rate, no brain activity, and absolutely no blood present in her brain at all. Nevertheless, after the procedure, she told the doctors that she had left her body and had an NDE. Not only could Pamela recall entire conversations among the surgical team, she went on to accurately describe the names, physical appearances, and locations of everyone who was in the room at the time of her operation, even those who had not yet arrived until after she was completely dead. She described the procedure in vivid detail, and even the appearance of the specialized tool used in the operation, which was only visible during the time of her death.[26]

Dr. Janice Holden has compiled a list of more than 100 similar cases in which patients have ascertained information during the experience that was later confirmed to be true,[27] and I've discovered many more smaller, anecdotal cases in my own research. Both the earliest NDE researchers, such as Dr. Sabom, and more contemporary researchers, such as Dr. Sartori, saw this phenomenon as incredibly challenging to their materialistic worldviews, and described in their publications the lengths to which they went in their attempts to find a natural explanation. Miller summarizes for us that Dr. Sabom, for example, set up a control group of patients who did not have an NDE and asked them to describe what they thought happened during the time of

---

[26] Michael Sabom. Light & Death: One Doctor's Fascinating Account of Near-Death Experiences. 1998.

[27] Holden, Janice. The Handbook of Near-Death Experiences. 2009. p194.

their death. Their responses were vague, generalized, and often incorrect, more in line with the portrayals in movies and television. However, when NDE patients were surveyed, the answers were very specific to the individual situation. One patient described receiving a shot in the groin, which was accurate for his own procedure, but not common practice for cardiac arrest resuscitation. In fact, Dr. Sabom said that the details of these accounts from NDE patients were so precise, and so accurate, that *he could have used the taped interviews to teach other physicians.* Dr. Sartori did her own independent study on the subject and also established a very clear distinction between the vague and erroneous guesses of most people, and the hyper-realistic, and individualized descriptions provided by NDE patients. It was clear to the professionals who spoke to these patients and studied hundreds of these accounts first-hand that it was impossible to explain away this phenomenon with mere "good guesses."

So, unlike dreams or visions produced in the mind of the individual, NDEs show a remarkable consistency in recurring characters, themes, and events, regardless of the age, race, or worldview of the patients, and regardless of any preconceived beliefs about the afterlife. While no one is convinced that their dreams represent real experiences outside of their body, NDE patients return to life convinced that what they have experienced is an objective reality beyond our material world, and the *overwhelming* majority of patients subsequently adopt a belief in an afterlife. Unlike dreams which are often interrupted mid-sentence, NDEs almost always have closure, ending with a voluntary or mandatory return to the physical body. And unlike

33

the vague, erroneous guesses of most patients, hundreds of NDE survivors have ascertained and reported incredibly specific details and facts that would have been impossible for them to know unless they actually experienced what they claim.

Some have attempted to explain this degree of consistency through shared physical stressors on the mind or body at the time of death, common to all humanity, which therefore produce common elements in the vision. Although this theory might be able to explain a few of the commonalities, I wouldn't expect a shared physical stressor in the body to result in telepathy as a common mode of communication, nor could this theory address the lack of interruption or the veridical perception of the survivors. We would need to invoke significantly more assumptions to address these other phenomena. So I find this theory to be lacking in explanatory power.

Similarly, some have claimed that veridical perception is all smoke and mirrors, that NDErs observe conversations audibly despite the appearance of death, that Pamela Reynolds just saw the surgical instruments before being put under, and I've even seen some people claim that Vicki Umipeg is lying and that she can actually see more than she lets on. But this theory is sorely inadequate to explain how Pamela Reynolds could have heard medical staff conversations when her brain wasn't even registering the 100dB clicks pounding directly in her ears, or seen the locations of staff in the operating room with an inoperable brain and her eyes taped over. Similarly, this theory has no explanation for instances of children meeting deceased siblings or sudden knowledge of a parent's past relationships. Such things were not discussed in the vicinity of the body at the time of death, so could not have been perceived subconsciously. Nor could this knowledge have come about through psychotropic drugs or stimulation of certain parts of the brain during death. Simply stated, these theories would require significantly more assumptions than a straightforward interpretation of NDE accounts.

So rather than gaslighting NDE survivors, I believe the least ad hoc approach to NDEs is to take them at face value and trust the survivors' testimonies. Like the earliest researchers on the subject, who actually spoke to the survivors and weighed these accounts against their medical expertise, who set out to explain them through natural means, and yet subsequently abandoned their materialistic worldviews and adopted a belief in an afterlife, I too am convinced that the best explanation of NDEs is the genuine truth of an out of body experience, an objective reality beyond our material universe, a life after death.

3

In Distress

When I think of influential films from my childhood that I'm really looking forward to sharing with my kids on a future Friday Family Movie Night, one that quickly rises to the top of the list is The Matrix. The story, the action, the cinematography...it was truly a groundbreaking film. I still remember coming home from the cinema and reenacting all the fight scenes with my siblings. It's the kind of film that will leave you thinking about it for weeks after you see it.

Slight spoiler here, but sometimes I wonder what it would have felt like to be Neo in that moment of awakening in the real world for the first time. To realize that he was now in a realm that he had never known, never experienced, and didn't even know existed. New sights, new sounds, new textures and smells. I imagine that fear would be one of the first emotions to arise in me, perhaps apprehension at navigating uncertain and unfamiliar terrain, and possibly terror at the images and creatures encountered for the first time.

Understandably, some NDE patients report similar reactions to their experiences, forming what has become known as a distressing NDE, often called a "DNDE." Although some patients may experience similar features and characteristics of pleasant NDEs, they react to them with fear - fear of the unknown, of leaving life unfinished, or simply fear of what happens next. I think fear is a natural reaction to new and unknown experiences, especially something as drastic as a life after death, so it is certainly an understandable reaction.

However, scholars Greyson and Bush have identified[28] another pattern of distressing NDE in which the NDEr was fully aware and conscious but existed in a void of nothingness. Since distressing NDEs are far less common, and have not been subjected to as much scholarly analysis as have pleasant NDEs, I believe the best way to understand DNDEs is to go straight to the source. What follows are the words of survivors who experienced this type of distressing NDE.

"The next thing I know I am in a black void. Completely conscious and more aware than I have ever been. I was not in my body. I was in a void. It was completely black and I had never felt so alone. There was no floor, walls, or light of any kind. It felt like I was falling but without wind or any other senses. I reflected on my life but in a way without any images in my mind. It was self-reflection with a sort of inner dialog with myself. I have never felt so

---

[28] Bruce Greyson & Nancy Evans Bush. Distressing Near-Death Experiences. Psychiatry Interpersonal & Biological Processes. March 1992.

alone or disconnected." This man went on to say that all he felt during the experience was extreme sadness.[29]

"I was aware of being somewhere else. Somewhere not where my physical body was. There was complete darkness, but more than darkness as in absence of light. It felt like nothingness. I looked around hoping to find a light or some loving presence, but there was nothing. The most absolute nothing I could imagine. I began to panic and the fear I felt was like nothing I have experienced before or after. The realization that there was nothing there, no light at the end of the tunnel, nothing. I was absolutely alone." [30]

"I suddenly found myself alone. In a dismal, gray immensely huge, foggy space, I was alone. I felt an overwhelming fear growing up inside me - I felt foul, spoiled, overcome with shame. Why I hadn't done more when I'd had the chance? The opportunity to change things for the better was now over and I'd missed it. The sense of remorse was overwhelming. A knowledge filled me—here in this horrible empty space—there was no possibility

---

[29] https://www.nderf.org/Experiences/1carl_s_nde.html
[30] https://www.nderf.org/Experiences/1connie_f_nde.html

for change. I felt so remorseful; I'd missed my chance." [31]

How terrifying it must feel to be conscious, to be "more aware" than at any other time in your life, to feel alive, to remember everything from your life, and yet to find absolutely nothing but a void. There are many who die and simply don't remember anything from the time of their death - it's simply lost time. However, what we see in the instances described above is not the case of lost time; it is a case of complete awareness of the passage of time, and a fatalistic fear and sadness that the present state will remain forever with no hope of change.

DNDE survivors report feelings of remorse, regret, terror, and loneliness - absolutely nothing like the pleasant NDEs described in the previous chapter. If NDEs are supposed to reveal some kind of spiritual truth to us, to help us understand the afterlife, then there certainly must be more to the story than just peace and love in the presence of the Being of light.

While the thought of conscious awareness of an isolated existence in a completely empty void is terrifying in and of itself, there is actually a third and even more terrifying pattern of distressing NDE described by Greyson and Bush. In these reports, NDErs encounter hellish beings or apparitions, they may exist in desolate darkness or agonizing brightness, it might be freezing cold, it might be scalding hot, sometimes it is utterly silent, at other times it is unbearably loud. Survivors report fear, pain, and even violence.

---

[31] https://www.nderf.org/Experiences/1ann_m_nde.html

Again, the research into distressing NDEs is limited in coverage and scope, so we will go straight to the source. What follows are the words of survivors who have had truly terrifying NDE experiences. Each is cited with a link to a page where you can read more about their story and the responses they gave to additional questions about the experience. I suggest you take your time here. And just a warning, these accounts can be intense and graphic, so prepare yourself.

> "I was then sucked downward into an unending tunnel or a vortex. It was very dark and there were red and orange flames everywhere. I was aware that I was dying and was frantic, but could not escape and come back or wake up. There was the strongest emotional and spiritual feeling of being oppressed in every possible way. It is almost unexplainable how much emotional pain I felt. It was almost as if every negative feeling I had ever felt in my life were being forced on me at once. Flashes of my past and terrible choices and mistakes I had made flew by me. I also saw faces of my family members, they were all crying. I knew I was going to hell, and it was a million times worse than I had ever imagined. There was no physical pain but I was being tortured emotionally for everything wrong I had ever done in life. In the spiritual world, this seemed to go on for many years, yet I was somehow aware that it was only minutes on earth. I remember being sorry for

all the things I had done and having complete regret." [32]

"I lost consciousness and then I felt like a fight within my body and then an escape towards a black tunnel, which had bronze colored stripes, at an ever increasing speed. There were unexpected bifurcations inside the tunnel; I turned to the right, went straight for some time and then changed directions again. I felt as if I was disintegrating inside the tunnel, i.e. my body lost consistency and I felt that the tunnel completely wrapped around me. I felt dizziness and was moving in spirals inside the tunnel. It is something indescribable. After a blow, I found myself in a viscous sea of mud. There were many people with me and we were trying to escape from it but could not. I was completely desperate; these people were suffering a lot; they were in torment." [33]

"I felt as though I were being suctioned and blown downwards...I reached a lake of blood and there was rotten burnt flesh. The smell of putrid flesh was unbearable. Holes would open in the earth at every step and horrible worms would come up. I raised my eyes and saw a man bending down and a demon raping him... and the demon was donkey-headed.

[32] https://www.nderf.org/Experiences/1ellen_f_probable_nde.html
[33] https://www.nderf.org/Experiences/1rachelle_g_nde.html

To the right I saw the anus of a giant that was defecating demons... To the left I saw people dancing... they wanted to stop but the demons did not let them." [34]

"I began hearing voices that got louder and louder and louder. Eventually, it was a loud ruckus all around me, but coming from below where I had been lying on a bed. I was still inside of a pitch-black void, but now I began to feel my r (*sic*) limbs. I was being [grabbed] by my legs, calves, and ankles, as Beings were trying to pull me downwards. Although I had been lying down on a bed before, it now felt as if I were upright and floating in space. I was not standing on anything. It seemed to me that the Beings below me were trying to pull me downwards to where they were because they were angry and tortured souls who wanted me to feel just as badly as they did. I remember feeling terrified. It was so dark and I could not see anything below me, so it was hard to figure out what was going on. As they pulled me downwards toward them, I began to feel progressively colder. As the Beings pulled me into their midst, it seemed squishy and wet, as well as dark and cold. Meanwhile, the Beings all around me were ripping and tearing at me." [35]

---

[34] https://www.nderf.org/Experiences/1dario_f_nde.html
[35] https://www.nderf.org/Experiences/1onya_m_probable_nde.html

"I just remember it was pitch black. I couldn't see anything, but I could hear screaming and what sounded like big angry animals or devils. These were awful sounds. I can't describe the smell, but the closest would be that it smelled rancid at best. I was unable to move. I could feel claws and teeth tearing at my skin. I was being eaten and torn to pieces. The pain was unimaginable. But I didn't die. I couldn't scream, nor could I get away. I couldn't understand how I was still being torn apart. My arms had been ripped off several times and I could feel something eating my stomach. Yet, I didn't die. I just kept suffering." [36]

"I immediately descended as if in a speeding elevator car. My only sensation was that of being taken downward in total darkness, total silence. When the descent ended, I was in the deepest, darkest void I had ever experienced...I tried to see but could not. I began to hear noise and what I heard was extremely distressing and eventually unbearable. As the noise grew in intensity, I realized it was voices, the countless voices of many, many souls, saying nothing, only weeping and wailing. It was the most anguished, pathetic sound I had ever heard. With every passing moment, it grew until I

---

[36] https://www.nderf.org/Experiences/1kim_m_probable_nde.html

imagined their numbers were in the millions. It was unbearable." [37]

"I was in a huge black square with small white dots. Throughout the square, it was like I was in space. I was in the center and I couldn't see myself at the time, but I heard loud ear-piercing banging. It sounded far away, but with every bang, it was getting closer. I heard a loud voice say, 'This is how it began and how it will end.' I felt so alone and afraid. The word 'void' kept popping up in my mind. Everything was black, except the small white dots. One dot was right in front of me, but it seemed a million miles away. Then everything switched over and I was somewhere else. It was all...black again. I felt as if I was in space. Then I heard my name, over and over again. All around me were things like demons and monsters. It felt like they were trying to tear off my body parts...Then I was alone and afraid, back in the black square. The loud banging was getting closer and closer. It was so lonely and cold, I can't describe it. But again, the word 'void' was in my head. It was the loud voice that kept saying in between the banging, 'This is how it began and how it will end.' I kept feeling the loneliness, and it was so cold, so dark, and so loud. Finally, the bang was right beside me. Again, I heard

---

[37] https://www.nderf.org/Experiences/1cathleen_c_nde.html

the voice saying, 'This is how it began and how it will end.' There were no more white dots, no more voice. I just heard the continuous ear-piercing bang and I heard, 'You're done.'" [38]

"I fell into a deep, dark pit that seemed infinite in size. I was perplexed when this happened, and looked around to try to find out where I was. As I looked down, I couldn't see my body anymore. I was simply a form of consciousness with my ego intact. I did not have to breathe, nor did I have any difficulty thinking, as though I was experiencing some sort of 'super consciousness'. I eventually landed with a thud, which caused an excruciating pain to pass through my body. This void was the darkest black that I have ever seen in my life. It's as if there was no light whatsoever in this dimension. Even if a light were to shine in this void, the darkness would have completely devoured it. I could not see anything, but the sounds that I heard were absolutely horrendous. I could hear what seemed like trillions of people screaming and crying in pain. Even though there were trillions of voices, I could distinguish all of the voices separately in some sort of superimposed, horrendous screech. I wasn't scared, I was absolutely livid. I knew that this was where my fate rested, in this deep dark pit.

---

[38] https://www.nderf.org/Experiences/1ed_w_nde.html

Suddenly, in the twinkling of an eye, 150 foot flames manifested all around me. This roaring inferno seemed to be a million times hotter and more intense than the sun. The colors were unlike any I've ever seen in my lifetime. The reds, oranges, yellows and other indescribable colors were so intense that I had trouble recognizing. I tried frantically to escape this fiery pit, but each time I tried to climb the wall, I slipped and landed back at the bottom of the pit. It was as if the 'walls' (boundaries more so than walls, very difficult to explain) were made of some sort of supernatural ice with no friction whatsoever. Surprisingly, I did not feel the flames of this hellish pit, but was still horrified as I could hear the many screams of the innumerable souls condemned to this seemingly eternal fate. I could see nothing but flames surrounding me. I cried out in horror as the scene switched to a disturbingly hideous and disgusting demon who towered over me, quite similar to a skyscraper next to a human being. I got the impression that this being was made out of pure hate and terror. It struck a terror so deep within me, that I still find it absolutely impossible to describe fifteen years later. It seemed like this being was about to propel my very soul in to oblivion. Even though I realized that I was dead, I felt as though this being could destroy me yet again in a horrendously tragic way, forever." [39]

"Then everything went black and I could not see anything and all my [thoughts] were played back to me. Then wherever I was started to fill with fog. I then felt myself move along a hallway of darkness. Then I heard someone calling my name and telling me to come along. I was ok and this [was] where I was to call home. They were there to guide me home. I could feel something was not right and I wanted to go back the way I came but I was told that I could not go back my time on earth was done. I was to keep moving and I would see my mom soon. The voices keep telling me to move along with them and to keep up. I looked back I felt something bad was going to happen to me and that I need to go back the way I came. Every time I look back, the voices told me to keep up and keep moving. I told myself that enough was enough and I said that I did not want to go any further [than] where I was, till they told me where I was and where we were going. The voices said that we had reached our point. That I was where I need to be now. I then could smell what I thought was sulphur and death. Then the voices started to laugh and say that this is what my life caused me to have. I asked where

I was and what was going to happen next. The voices just laughed some more and repeated what I said. I thought to myself that I had to be in hell, because this was not what my sister said happened to her. This is not how she said heaven was like. Then I could hear my thoughts out loud. The voices then said that there was not heaven for me. That this was the heaven that was to be mine. Then one of the[m] said that it was feeding time. Then I felt like I was pushed back into a wall and my arms pinned back to the wall. I felt totally helpless and then I saw what looked like hair ball[s] with shark teeth come at me. I looked to my right side and saw that the voices were little monsters that were turning into the hairballs and back into monsters. They were the ugliest looking things I have seen and yet to see. They looked like snakes crossed with bats crossed with something that had horns. They had bodies that were like that of a snake and it had wings. [Their] arms and hands look like those of a bat. Their faces look like snakes and they had fangs like a bat and a snake. On the top of their heads, they had horns, but not like the horns of a bull or a ram. They had pointed horns but nothing that I could say was earthly. As they turned into hairballs, I asked what was happening to me. They laughed and told me to shut up and I could hear my feeling[s] out loud. Then they started coming at me and as they did, I felt sick to my stomach. I remember feeling why is this happening? Where is my mom and where is God? Then I felt them feeding on me. I looked down at what I thought was my body and parts [were] gone. I then looked at them and my body parts [were] in their mouths. Then one of them said 'We told you already that this is your heaven and we are your God.'" [40]

"I started to fall, faster and faster and faster. I felt like I had literally just dropped vertically and was headed towards this sort of black hole. It was so dark I felt I could cut it with a knife. Still falling, I began to hear screams, cries, agonizing pain, horrible, horrible laughing and the most putrid smell you could ever imagine, then the blackness turned into fire, and I was falling towards a huge furnace. Fire began to consume me. I started screaming. I didn't know where my sound was going but I knew I was screaming hard. Landing on my back, I suddenly crashed to what seemed like rocks and felt a horrible pain all over my body or whatever this new form was. Opening my eyes I suddenly realized I wasn't alone because creatures, things of some sort of distorted form started to grasp at me, one by one they grabbed me and started to drag me towards what seemed like huge black gates. I began kicking and screaming, yelling

---

[40] https://www.nderf.org/Experiences/1joe_g_nde.html

at the top of my lungs for Allah or Buddha or God
-- whoever I could remember hearing about in
Religious Education classes to help me, but still
nothing came. I remember one giant creature began
to rip at the skin on my back with what seemed like
his sharp nails, another began to tear at my hair so
hard I felt the urge to throw up. Another kicked me
down and started standing on my chest laughing,
teasing me about personal issues he seemed to know
about me. Such as my mother dying at birth, my
sister in prison and my friend Gareth driving the car
that had killed me. I so remember the smell, it was
so vile like rotting flesh and burnt hair. Their raspy
laughs and taunts at me were almost drowned out
by the roar of the flames around me. I suddenly saw
before me people running and screaming, a group
of children no younger than twelve years old crying;
each one being terrorized and literally pulled apart
by these malevolent beings. I definitely remember
suddenly seeing Gareth, (the guy in the car with
me) -- he was hung upside down with nails driven
into his hands and feet, almost like Jesus on the
Cross (I had remembered reading about that in
class a few weeks ago). The creatures began
whipping him simultaneously, all chanting in a
language I really didn't understand. Fire had now
consumed what he was nailed to and the flesh on
his hands and chest and head had already begun to
melt and peel. I looked at his face, he was

TERRIFIED!!!! He began crying uncontrollably pleading with them to stop. My body or soul or whatever you want to call it suddenly began to burn badly from the fire spread on this ground. I suddenly cried out again, 'God please help me.' I suddenly realized that the more I cried out God's name, the more they tried to hurt me, the angrier they got, the more agitated and frustrated they became. 'God please,' I finally begged seconds before deciding to give up and suddenly a great suction tore me from their grip and started to carry me back through the tunnel. I suddenly awoke to the sound of a female doctor's voice." [41]

~ Take a Minute to Catch your Breath ~

Terrifying. Truly terrifying experiences. It's no wonder that DNDEs are believed to be underreported and only account for about 15% of all reported NDE experiences. Even if someone did experience such a horrific reality, I imagine they would feel judged as deserving of such a terrible fate in the afterlife; or maybe others just want to forget the experience entirely. But regardless of the rarity of these distressing NDEs, they are in fact a reality of the NDE phenomenon, and we must therefore take them into account in our investigation and development of an appropriate framework through which to understand them. I applaud the courage of the men and women who have brought these accounts

---

[41] https://www.nderf.org/Experiences/1meg_a_nde.html

to us, and I hope that we can learn from them and find answers, both for past survivors, and for others in the future.

As with pleasant NDEs, although the accounts vary from person to person, we do find common themes and elements in DNDEs: darkness, the void, flames, demons, ominous sounds, and putrid smells. We'll take a closer look at some of these phenomena in Chapter 5, but while these are fresh in your mind, I'd like to highlight a few points of interest. First, note that the demonic creatures often had an awareness of the individual's entire life, taunting them with painful memories from their lives. Second, note that scenes and environments could change in an instant. Finally, note that the NDErs all felt trapped, unable to escape, and unable to awaken from the nightmare of their new reality.

Visit the links in the footnotes and read the full accounts and the responses they provide to the questionnaire. As with pleasant NDEs, DNDE survivors know that the experience was real, and many spend the rest of their lives trying to understand what that means.

But questions abound. If pleasant NDEs have so many similarities and common features, why are there so many differences in distressing NDE accounts? Why do some people simply exist in a void while others are literally torn apart and consumed by demonic creatures? Why are there distressing NDEs at all? Why do some people feel peace, love, and comfort while others feel terror and isolation? Why do some people get to visit with deceased loved ones while others find themselves accompanied only by demonic creatures? If the Being of light in pleasant NDEs is supposed to be some sort of loving deity, as some would claim, then how could this Being justify the horrific treatment of DNDErs and the other people they observed during their experiences?

Approximately one year into my NDE research, after wrestling with these questions and struggling to reconcile competing and contradictory truth claims, I finally discovered what I believe to be the answer. I believe that one particular NDE account opens the door for us to resolve these contradictions and uncertainties. Through the details reported by this NDE survivor, I believe we can build a framework that will help us to identify and categorize all NDEs in a logical and consistent manner. When you have emotionally recovered from the horror of this chapter, we'll spend the next chapter reviewing this account and exploring the details that will help us establish and refine the framework.

4

A Land Best Forgotten

For my generation, few actors have filled the role of comic genius better than Jim Carrey. I can pretty much guarantee that if you spend enough time with me, or any of my peers, a quote from Dumb and Dumber will find its way into relevant conversation. But for all of the slapstick comedy that made him famous in Ace Ventura and The Mask, Carrey decided to try his hand at a more dramatic role in The Truman Show.

~ Spoiler Alert ~

The premise of the movie is that Truman, an unwanted child, was adopted by a television production company who built an entire world around him to create the ultimate reality television program. Everything in his life was part of the set, everyone in his life was part of the cast. And the entire world knew the truth about this mysterious reality, except Truman himself. Applicable to our current investigation, the show's creator, played by Ed Harris, exclaims at one point in the film, "we accept the reality of the world with which we're presented."

However, as the movie progresses, Truman becomes increasingly convinced that something is wrong with his world. He begins to notice others watching and following him, he becomes perplexed when a spotlight falls from the sky, and he even overhears radio communication between the cast and crew. Truman decides he must escape. Courageously facing the fears instilled in him by the production, he commandeers a boat and sets sail for what he thinks is Fiji. To his surprise, however, he comes to a screeching halt when the bowsprit of his sailboat punches a hole in a wall painted to look like the sky.

The confusion, the anger, the disbelief - Carrey expertly captures the emotion of the moment and helps us to understand exactly what it might feel like to suddenly discover that the reality of the world with which we are presented may not actually be the reality of the world beyond the wall.

~ END OF SPOILERS ~

In a similar way, the NDE account that helped me formulate the framework through which I now view all NDEs tells a similar story of breaking through the wall of an artificial reality to discover a completely different reality on the other side. This account is unique in that it is one of a small number of NDEs that consist of both pleasant and distressing experiences. And I believe that this account gives us sufficient insight into the nature of both types of NDEs to serve as a starting point for the framework. So before we fully develop the framework itself, let's take a closer look at this man's story.

~ BRYAN'S STORY ~

Bryan Melvin was a self-proclaimed hardened atheist, *absolutely certain* of his lack of belief in any kind of deity or god.[42] In his book, he recounts for us moments of inquisition by his religious family members and the arguments he used against them whenever questions about his worldview would arise:

> "God does not exist because of all the evil in the world, and if He were so great, powerful, just, merciful, He would put a stop to it, but since evil continues, how can God exist?"

> "[A]ll religions lead to the same end. It did not matter what one believed because all roads lead to the same destination."

Like many of his peers, Bryan spent much of his early twenties biding his time throughout the week, waiting for the next weekend kegger to begin. Music, friends, booze, repeat. Bryan really was living his best life. If, for some reason, he actually woke up early on a Sunday morning, he recalls spending that time

---

[42] Bryan's full account can be found in his book: Melvin, B W. *A Land Unknown: Hell's Dominion.* Xulon Press. 2005.

mocking the Christians walking down the street outside his duplex in Tucson, Arizona as they obediently marched into the local church. Sheep! Or so he thought at the time.

Bryan was working construction as an electrician; not the easiest job on those hot Tucson summer days. One afternoon on the site, he noticed a water cooler in the bed of one of the pickup trucks. He grabbed it and chugged a nice long blast of what he expected to be ice-cold, refreshing water, only to discover a rancid aftertaste burning in his mouth and throat. It turns out the water in this particular cooler was not potable and was ripe with all kinds of disgusting and dangerous bacteria.

Over the course of the next few days, Bryan would contract cholera from the contaminated water, though the stubborn young buck decided he would just tough it out and bear through the stomach pains and high fever, unaware of the severity of his illness. That weekend, his roommates had planned a road trip, but Bryan, still very ill, decided he would need to stay home to recover while they embarked on the adventure.

Lying in bed, trying to stay warm under a heavy blanket, feeling as if his stomach was being sliced by razor blades, chest heaving to catch a breath, he noticed that the blurred image of his bedroom suddenly became clear, even though his glasses still remained on his bedside table. The pain in his stomach had subsided, but his chest was no longer moving the covers in a rhythmic, breathing motion. He rolled over and, to his surprise, found himself floating above his bed, face to face with his own dead body.

Slowly, Bryan began to float up and out through the roof of his duplex, passing straight through the walls and ceiling as if they weren't even there. On his way up, he noticed a dirty thumbprint within a crease in the ceiling texture, and found it a little odd that he had never noticed it from the ground below. His ascent continued, high above his neighborhood, high above his city, and into a dark tunnel overhead. The tunnel terminated in a small light in the distance which, as he approached, turned out to be a Being made of a light that shined with such intensity that it fully illuminated the otherwise pitch black encompassing atmosphere. In awe of what stood before him, Bryan fell to his knees, knowing for the first time that his atheistic worldview had been completely wrong.

The Being of light gave Bryan a life review, showing him every scene of his life, from birth to death, and explained how *It* had been with him through it all, even when it didn't feel that way. Through a telepathic form of communication, the Being conveyed Its love for Bryan and the compassion it felt for him, despite the numerous evil actions that were on full display in his life review.

As Bryan knelt before this Being, It told him that his journey was only just beginning and that he had been granted an opportunity to see something entirely different. Although Bryan was still uncertain of the meaning behind the words, the Being told him that he would soon arrive at a land which It described as "best forgotten, but not left unseen." Likely in an attempt to offer comfort or reassurance, It said that the journey would be temporary and that It would return him to his present location when he had seen what needed to be seen.

Bryan watched in amazement as the Being opened a door, behind which was found a portal of sorts - a swirling vortex of dark, earthen colors. As if he were completely weightless, Bryan was lifted and carried to the vortex, and then sucked inside. It propelled him forward, twisting and turning along the way, until a faint yellowish light began to emerge at its end, drawing closer and closer as he continued speeding through the vortex.

The vortex dropped him into an entirely different location. Under the yellowish light of a sunset sky, Bryan took a moment to take in his new surroundings, utterly confused by what had just transpired. He was standing in a beautiful field, under the warm light of a sky one might expect to find in a serene landscape painting. A group of people emerged from a nearby house on the hill and ran to greet Bryan with expressions of love and excitement. Numerous friends and family members rushed to his side to shower him with warm embraces and welcome him to Paradise.

But something was amiss. The eyes of his friends and family were somehow unfamiliar, somehow "wrong," though he couldn't quite put his finger on the discrepancy. Also, Bryan spotted some in the crowd who were still alive, which only added to his skepticism about what was happening. While some of the people tried to distract him and draw his attention away, others instantly transformed into different people, seemingly attempting to assuage the growing questions in Bryan's mind. Yet, Bryan persisted. He wanted to know what was really happening and why.

At that moment, the people instantly transformed into hellish, demonic creatures. Bryan describes them as reptilian, but with some human characteristics. With raptor-like claws on their feet and hands, and shark-like teeth. Their toxic breath was so foul that it bent the surrounding light like a mirage over an asphalt road on a hot summer day. Their skin was yellowish-green and appeared moldy or rotten, and their short, stocky stature reminded him of Tolkien's Orcs.

In screams of rage and fury, they lunged at Bryan, attempting to tear his skin and rip off his limbs, but were unable to touch him or harm him in any way. In a barely-discernible form of communication, one of the creatures begrudgingly told Bryan to follow it, as he had been given permission to see this place as it really was. The creature trudged towards the horizon, and reached its hand through it, as if piercing a projector screen and interrupting the virtual image. Bryan followed the creature through what felt like an opening in a curtain, leaving behind the empty field beneath a yellow sunset, and entering into an entirely new domain.

Once beyond the veil, Bryan discovered the true reality of his situation. He had just emerged from what amounted to a prison cell; a cube 3 to 4 meters on all sides. The beautiful field beneath a serene sunset had been nothing more than a virtual environment, a projected experience created by the walls of his cell. In reality, he was standing on a wide, dirty road, that slowly spiraled downward as you traversed it in a clockwise direction, with a massive void in the center, as if the entire structure was constructed like a spiral staircase or circular car ramp. The diameter of the curvature was so massive that the downward slope was almost imperceptible. Standing at the inner edge of the road, one could look up and down and find countless spiral layers in both directions, revealing the immense size of this facility. Opposite the central pit, the outer edge of the road was bordered by a wall of cubes, each similar to his own, stacked 6 high and directly adjacent to each other. The cubes were innumerable.

Each cube was somewhat translucent and, from the outside, one could see what was happening inside. In fact, in a kind of double vision, Bryan could see not only the actual reality of what was happening inside the cube, but also the virtual experience perceived by the person. Additionally, as he looked inside the cubes, Bryan could see the entire history of the person inside, not only in life, but also during their time in the cell. As the person moved, the floor beneath them moved like a 2-dimensional treadmill, keeping them centered in the cube regardless of their perceived reality. In anguish, Bryan watched as one person after another arrived in their own individual cube, some appearing instantly, others via a vortex like himself, and still others through an ominous network of corridors. But the tour had only just begun. His reptilian tour guide bid Bryan to follow.

As they approached a seam between two adjacent cubes, the cube walls receded just enough for them to pass through, revealing more cubes behind them. It turned out that the cubes along the edge of the road were only the first of many layers deep - there were considerably more cubes than Bryan had first realized. As they made their way through the maze of passageways between the cubes, Bryan recorded for us many of the things he saw happening inside.

A woman sat alone on a beach drawing circles in the sand. A man sat by himself in a small boat trying to catch a fish. A man was teased and mocked by other guests at a costume party. Another man who sought only fame and fortune in life, sat alone under the hot sun of a barren desert. Some cubes were engulfed in flames. Others contained people who believed they were in Paradise, accompanied by family and friends, or surrounded by beautiful gardens and terrain, and only much later did the boredom and isolation begin to drive thoughts of fear, anger, and guilt into their minds. Another former professor stood alone in front of an empty classroom endlessly writing, "I know it all" on a chalkboard. A woman stood alone on a tree-lined avenue in 19th century France. A man who once sent an innocent business rival to prison sat alone in what looked like the cell where his rival rotted away his life. A woman who sacrificed many children to her gods was haunted by visions of those children and mauled and tormented by these demonic creatures. An avowed Satanist in life sat in a dark room lit only by candles while these demonic creatures taunted him for believing their lies. A man from ancient Central America who performed many live sacrifices to the gods in his lifetime found himself tied to the altar and felt the pain of that stone knife plunge endlessly into his body. A woman who practiced a religion of worshiping mother nature was continually attacked while these creatures mockingly told her to pray to the stones for deliverance. A man who lusted after women and then killed and buried them on his property continually experienced what it felt like to be buried alive. A man who committed countless crimes against humanity as a Nazi in World War II felt first-hand the physical and emotional pain he caused others: the grief of watching your child get shot, the shame of being raped, the fear of being buried alive, the pain of being burned alive, and numerous other atrocities he inflicted on innocent victims in his life.

Again and again, Bryan witnessed people tormented by extreme boredom and isolation, others reaping what they had sown, tormented by their own guilt over their actions in life, and still others being tortured by demonic creatures in various nightmarish scenarios. At times, he had to look away, disgusted by the horrors being experienced by these captive human souls.

Oddly, Bryan notes that the demonic creatures could enter and exit these cubes and move freely throughout this entire domain. Inside the cubes, they could appear in any form to the inhabitants. Some appeared as the reptilian orc-like creatures that they are. Some took the form of humans interacting with the captive person. Others took the form of passive objects in the room. Still others would simply disappear from view, waiting for the right time to pounce and invoke the greatest amount of terror. They could appear as giants, or the size of insects. And they could physically interact with the captive human, grabbing them, moving them, throwing them around like a rag-doll, even "eating" them and then regurgitating them. They would bury people alive, and tear apart their flesh, they even crucified a man who lived as an ancient Roman soldier. Yet the people never found the release of death, only constant torture.

Bryan's guide led him to an open cube with what looked like a dentist's chair in the center, and tried to persuade him to step inside. They told him he was home and would now enjoy an eternity together with them. Yet, as he stood there, paralyzed with fear, a bright light began to grow behind him, and the creatures began to flee. The Being of light appeared and picked Bryan up. It carried him to the edge of the cube wall that bordered the wide, dusty road, and then levitated up through the center of the structure. Together, they returned to Bryan's original cube where a vortex arrived and took them back to where they had started. The Being communicated with Bryan for some time and then left him with a single question before sending him back to his body:

> "God grants you life; will you now walk with God, decreasing ugliness in the land, as an extension of the Master's Hands? Or will you walk away from God ensuring ugliness remains where you trod?"

Fortunately for Bryan, his roommates had asked their duplex neighbor to check on him before they departed on their road trip. As Bryan began to awaken, returning to the pain and blurred vision of his material body, his neighbor found him and drove him to a nearby hospital, where he was treated for cholera and recovered. For the longest time, Bryan lived in constant fear that he had actually died and was now trapped in a virtual reality inside his own cube. Or was it all a dream? His thoughts raced day and night, preventing him from sleeping.

Until one day, he climbed a ladder and put his face up against the ceiling above his bed. There, in a crease in the ceiling texture, hidden from the view below, was that dirty thumbprint, exactly where he remembered it. Though the experience felt entirely real to him, this only further convinced him that what he had encountered was not just a dream or a delirious vision, it was real; the Being of light was real, that land, though certainly best forgotten, was real, and definitely best not left unseen.

~ REVELATIONS FROM THE LAND BEST FORGOTTEN ~

I'll discuss how Bryan's account can point us toward a new framework through which to view all NDEs in the next chapter, but I'd like to highlight a few important notes here while the story is still fresh in your mind.

First, Bryan's story shows us that NDEs do not necessarily represent the final fate of the individual, as he was exposed to both a pleasant and distressing NDE. And I have found at least one child who experienced both of these extremes as well, but in the opposite order. He described a vortex, what he called a tornado lying flat on the ground, and a hellish creature, with green, decaying skin, hook-like claws on its hands and feet, and large pointed teeth. He was then plucked from this hellish environment and carried to be with the Being of light and deceased family members.[43]

So we should not look at NDEs as personal indicators of individual destiny, but rather as individualized experiences, designed to reveal some aspect of spiritual truth to be shared with the rest of us. We should avoid the temptation to judge any individual for the experience they were given, and instead view them as data points from which we can learn a little more about life after death.

Second, there are many NDErs whose experience is pleasant and beautiful, and they return with this new-found anticipation of dying and returning to that beautiful afterlife of which they

---

[43] Richard Bonenfant. A Child's Encounter with the Devil: An Unusual Near-Death Experience with Both Blissful and Frightening Elements. Journal of Near Death Studies, winter 2001. p87-99.

have only briefly glimpsed. However, DNDEs are indicative of an afterlife that is most certainly not all sunshine and roses. Bryan witnessed thousands, perhaps millions, of human souls confined in a cubic prison cell in the afterlife. He even witnessed some who were deceived into believing they were in Paradise, and experienced that enchanting deception first-hand. So it is in our best interest to take the time in this life to understand why the afterlife is beautiful and loving for some, and full of isolation, torment, or worse for others. Otherwise we, or those we love, might sadly wake up in that land best forgotten when our present life finally expires. It is to this end that I have devoted much of the remainder of this book, starting with framework development in the next chapter.

~ NOTE ~

If you have the time, I highly recommend reading Bryan's book, "A Land Unknown: Hell's Dominion". You can find both Kindle and paperback versions on Amazon. He includes so many more details of his journey, describing the sights, sounds, smells, and feel of the Land Best Forgotten. He includes conversations with the demonic creatures that roam the area, revealing their own thoughts and perceptions of the situation, and offers detailed descriptions of the various beings residing in that place. It is an eye-opening, and a heart-wrenching first-hand account of what may possibly be the fate of many.

5

THE FRAMEWORK

The Usual Suspects easily takes its place among the best mystery films in Hollywood history, at least in my opinion. Among the hundreds of movies that influenced me during my formative years, this was one of the few movies whose promotional poster graced the walls of my childhood bedroom. Not because it was filled with big-budget action sequences or humorous one-liners, but because the movie itself is as mysterious as the events that unfold in the story. In fact, I enjoy this movie so much that I'm not even going to include a proper spoiler here for fear that my kids might read this before I get to show it to them on a future Friday Family Movie Night. But one profound revelation of the story that will be familiar to anyone who has seen it is that if we simply turn around and look at the evidence from a different perspective, we may discover a truth more profound than we ever expected.

Up to this point, I have been feeding you the evidence, exposing you to years of reading and research, and taking you deeper into the first-hand accounts of NDE survivors. And it is at this point in our journey that I invite you to turn around and look at this evidence from a new perspective. We've uncovered stories of hope, love, and forgiveness, as well as feelings of anger, isolation, and terror. Now it's time to develop a perspective on all of this evidence; one that can unify these stories, build on their underlying commonalities, and provide context for each and every near-death experience.

For years, many NDE researchers have simply taken each NDE at face value, accepting the information revealed by each one as objectively true, despite their internal contradictions. Others, like Atwater, deny the objective reality of these experiences and relegate the entire event to a creation of the mind, formulated by the individual's psychological state and preconceived expectations[44]. Here I would like to offer a different perspective. And I believe that if you will simply turn around and take an honest look, it will provide you with a deeper understanding of the underlying truth revealed by this amazing phenomenon. So let's begin our discourse by reviewing some of the common threads that bind many of these experiences together, beginning with the distressing side of NDEs.

~ THE JOURNEY ~

Although not all distressing NDEs describe the journey between the place of death on Earth and the other location where the distressing experience takes place, there is a common idea that

---

[44] Atwater, P.M.H. (1992). Is there a hell? Surprising observations about the near-death experience. Journal of Near-Death Studies, 10, 149-160.

the experience took place somewhere else, away from the body. This woman[45] explicitly states that she was fully aware of being somewhere else, not with her body. This idea is further implied in the numerous other cases where people describe falling into a dark tunnel or vortex.[46] [47] [48] [49] [50] [51]

This is interesting, first, because the evidence seems to indicate that, like pleasant NDEs, distressing NDEs also take place elsewhere. They are not merely visions or apparitions in and around the brain or body. Second, the direction of downward travel to the destination is interesting because most pleasant NDErs describe their journey as "upward," not downward. Third, it's interesting to note that many DNDE survivors offer a common description of this vortex as dark but striped or swirling with earthen reds, yellows, oranges, and greens.

However, not all DNDE survivors arrive via a swirling vortex. Many simply appear in the void or a new space.[52] [53] [54] And others seem to arrive by being led down a hallway of sorts.[55] But neither of these elements appear in many pleasant NDEs, if any at all.

---

[45] https://www.nderf.org/Experiences/1connie_f_nde.html

[46] https://www.nderf.org/Experiences/1ellen_f_probable_nde.html

[47] https://www.nderf.org/Experiences/1cathleen_c_nde.html

[48] https://www.nderf.org/Experiences/1tony_m_probable_nde.html

[49] https://www.nderf.org/Experiences/1meg_a_nde.html

[50] https://www.nderf.org/Experiences/1alessandra_p_nde.html

[51] https://www.nderf.org/Experiences/1dario_f_nde.html

[52] https://www.nderf.org/Experiences/1carl_s_nde.html

[53] https://www.nderf.org/Experiences/1ann_m_nde.html

[54] https://www.nderf.org/Experiences/1onya_m_probable_nde.html

[55] https://www.nderf.org/Experiences/1joe_g_nde.html

So the patterns in mode of transportation, the direction of travel, and manner of arrival are all entirely different from the patterns found in pleasant NDEs. Then is it reasonable to conclude that the realm of distressing NDEs is entirely different from that of pleasant NDEs, that people travel to it differently, and that therefore the experience should be expected to be entirely different? I believe so.

~ The Void ~

Recall the second type of Distressing NDE categorized by Greyson and Bush in Chapter 3 - those that take place in the complete isolation of the "void." In the accounts mentioned above, the void is described as the most absolute nothingness imaginable, in which a person feels more alone and disconnected than ever before in their entire life.

However, did you notice that many of the examples cited within the third type of DNDE also existed in a void at one point or another? Like this one[56] where the NDEr spent all her time in a pitch black void, but encountered horrible, ominous sounds and could feel demonic creatures grabbing at her from below, trying to pull her down into their midst. Or this one[57] where the woman felt the excruciating pain of being eaten alive and dismembered, but could see absolutely nothing but pitch black the entire time. Even this one,[58] with its terrifying sounds, ominous words, and horrible demonic creatures, took place in

---

[56] https://www.nderf.org/Experiences/1onya_m_probable_nde.html

[57] https://www.nderf.org/Experiences/1kim_m_probable_nde.html

[58] https://www.nderf.org/Experiences/1ed_w_nde.html

what the survivor repeatedly describes as the "void," a black square that invoked in him a sensation like floating in outer space. One Type-3 DNDE survivor even says, "The void was the darkest black that I have ever seen in my life."[59]

The fact that this void is consistent in both the second and third types of Greyson and Bush Distressing NDEs is an important fact that should not be overlooked. It is a common thread that links the experiences together and may therefore indicate some underlying commonality between the NDEs themselves. Not all DNDEs involving what we might call "demonic oppression" also mention a void, but could we conversely say that not all DNDEs occurring in a void involve demonic oppression?

What if those who spent their entire time in the void only fell into category two because these demonic creatures simply didn't visit them? After all, if any of the NDEs mentioned above hadn't encountered ominous sounds, or the sensation of being eaten or dismembered by demons, their experience would have consisted solely of the pitch black void. What if these two types of DNDEs are actually the exact same thing, except that some people are visited by demonic creatures, and others are not?

~ Discontinuous Surroundings~

The only problem with this theory is that not all Type-3 DNDEs actually take place in a void. However, if we look closely at the DNDE survivors' descriptions of their surroundings, I believe we can find a solution to this problem. In one account

---

[59] https://www.nderf.org/Experiences/1tony_m_probable_nde.html

cited earlier,[60] a woman landed in the void. However, in what she describes as the "twinkling of an eye," 150-foot flames appeared out of nowhere and completely engulfed her, but oddly these flames did not burn her. She then states that the scene immediately changed - the flames were gone and she was left cowering below a terrifying demon the size of a skyscraper. Another man[61] describes watching as the demonic creatures that were eating his body parts morphed between small hairballs and hideous hybrids of snakes and bats. And a different man[62] found himself in an odd western shoot-out with strange skeleton men when he was wounded and placed on the counter of a general store to rest. Then the scene went completely black and he found himself walking through a dark cave, emerging into a new room with massive pillars. As he walked slowly toward the new environment, the cave walls transformed from all black to overwhelming white. And the scenery of this man's NDE[63] changed instantly from a void to a view of the entire universe, and then again changed instantly to a field of oily colors.

So when we look more closely at some of these NDEs that don't quite fit the usual patterns of pleasant NDEs, one common thread we discover is a phenomenon I call "discontinuous surroundings." People are in one situation, and then in the twinkling of an eye, the scene changes. A pitch black void, to massive flames. A western town to a black cave. A bird's eye view of the universe, to a colorful earthly field. While pleasant NDE

---

[60] https://www.nderf.org/Experiences/1tony_m_probable_nde.html

[61] https://www.nderf.org/Experiences/1joe_g_nde.html

[62] https://www.nderf.org/Experiences/1alan_nde.html

[63] https://www.nderf.org/Experiences/1serge_d_nde.html

survivors report being able to travel rapidly, the descriptions provided here don't so much correspond to travel as to an instantaneous change of the surrounding environment. It's not the person who moves to different locations, but rather the appearance of the surrounding location changes around the person. So if that is the case, is it reasonable to conclude that the "void" is just another one of those appearances? Perhaps the void is the default appearance for the location, like a blank construct, and then these other scenes and locations simply manifest over the top? That's exactly what happened to the woman above who encountered 150-foot flames and a towering demon. She started in the void, unable to escape or leave, and then the scene changed around her.

But this woman's account provides us with two even more interesting details. First, she reports that she didn't feel the flames - they didn't burn her. This should tell us that the flames were not actually "real" in the sense that they could consume her body - they just *looked* real. Second, she reports that she tried to climb out of the pit in which she was trapped, but states that there were not actually any walls - only strange "boundaries" with absolutely no friction by which she could grab hold. This tells us that even in what appeared to be an endless black void, even in what appeared to be massive flames all around her, she was in fact confined inside a space with imperceptible barriers and had no means of escape.

Therefore, it seems to me that all of these DNDE accounts could take place within a similar place of confinement. A place with inescapable "boundaries," even if there were no visible walls. A place that could change its appearance to almost anything - a black void, a fiery furnace, a western town, the outer universe. A place where perceived reality is not exactly what it seems, where fire looks and sounds real and scary, but doesn't necessarily burn. This would further reinforce the idea that the second and third types of Greyson and Bush DNDEs are exactly the same. Some people encounter the void, others encounter strange scenery - like a western town or an oily field. Some people experience demonic oppression, others do not. Could it be, then, that every single distressing NDE occurs in a similar place of confinement?

~ Putting it all Together ~

While pleasant NDEs often describe a sensation of elevating upwards towards the Being of light, many DNDE accounts describe falling through a dark hole, or a twisted, swirling earthen-colored vortex to an entirely different location. And this is exactly what Bryan describes in his book - ascending through the roof of his duplex to meet the Being of light and then falling through a swirling vortex to arrive in the field under a setting sun. He confirms for us what we had inferred from the evidence, that the realm of pleasant NDEs with the Being of light is entirely different from that of distressing NDEs, and it would seem that the manner of one's arrival may help to determine in which realm the NDE occurs. He also noted that, while many people arrived in their cell via a vortex as he had done, others simply appeared in their cell, and still others arrived through an ominous network of hallways - the exact patterns that emerge in distressing NDEs.

While inside his cubic cell, Bryan experienced discontinuous changes of scenery as people instantly transformed into other people, consistent with other nonsensical discontinuities recorded in numerous DNDEs. But Bryan's experience diverged when he stepped out of his cell. And from his new perspective he witnessed countless others in their own cells, each living in their own personal Hell. Some utterly alone, others tormented by their actions in life, and some even under torture of visiting demonic creatures. So the question arises in my mind: was Bryan witnessing a subjective scene, his own version of a distressing NDE, but no more objectively real or ubiquitous than any other DNDE? Or could Bryan actually have been witnessing the individual afterlife experiences of thousands of other deceased people residing in that facility?

If the virtual reality created inside his cube could look like a beautiful field under a setting sun, could that reality also look like a pitch black void? Could it look like a barren wasteland? Or a beautiful garden? Could it appear as a lake of blood or a fiery pit? Do you remember the woman who wasn't burned by the 150-foot flames? Could it be that the flames were only a manifestation of the walls of her cube? Could that explain why she encountered "boundaries" that didn't appear to be walls and yet she was unable to climb out? If, as Bryan describes, the reality presented within each cube is entirely unique and isolated from all other cubes, could that explain why every DNDE is unique? Different environments, different scenarios, different characters, and even different forms of demonic torture?

If Bryan's demonic visitors could transform between different human appearances, could they not also appear as small balls of light, or inanimate objects such as a tree? Could they transform between hairballs and bat/snake hybrids as easily as they transformed between human forms? If, as Bryan noted, they could vanish from sight, would that give context to those DNDErs who could feel, but not see, the demons ripping them apart and eating them alive? And since Bryan describes many cubes in which there were no demonic visitors at all, could this explain those DNDEs, in the void or other distressing environments, which contain no demonic oppression?

All this to say, is it possible that every single distressing NDE we've covered thus far actually took place in its own individual cell in the Land Best Forgotten? Could it be that the void only looks like a void, just as Bryan's field only *looked* like a field? Could it be that the 150-foot flames only looked like flames, just as Bryan's sunset only *looked* like a sunset? Could it be that a DNDEr who spent their entire time alone in the void was actually sitting isolated in their own cell, cut off from the distressing experiences of those around them, sheltered from the demons who were either occupied elsewhere or unable to enter that particular cube? Could it be that these demonic visitors, whom Bryan describes as moving freely among the cubes, simply take on different forms and appearances and carry out different forms of torture on different people in different cubes? Could it be that DNDErs get only a small glimpse into a potentially infinite number of distressing realities that one might find inside a cube in the Land Best Forgotten, yet are fortunate enough to return to life with an opportunity to escape that fate at their final death? I have come to believe that the walls of the cubic cells in the Land Best Forgotten, and the virtual experience they provide for the person inside, can perfectly explain both the similarities and disparities across the full gamut of distressing NDEs, thereby unifying them as merely different manifestations of a perceived reality within a common state of confinement.

But could this also explain those strange NDE stories that don't quite fit into the dichotomy of pleasant or distressing? Could it be that, just as Bryan encountered demons posing as loved ones, DNDE survivors don't actually see or meet their loved ones, but are merely met by demons playing a role in a demented game of deception and torture? After all, Bryan witnessed a woman arrive in her cell showered with love and affection by a demon disguised as her grandma who told this woman to go enjoy the beautiful scenery of Paradise while she prepared her favorite dessert. Had she been revived at that moment, is it not likely that she would have found her NDE to be entirely pleasant? Is it not likely that we might have cataloged it as a pleasant NDE? Following this hypothesis to its logical conclusion, I have come to believe that many NDEs which may not feel entirely distressing may have also taken place in a cube in the Land Best Forgotten. And I believe there are telltale signs that can clue us in on what may be happening behind the scenes. Let's take a look at a few more NDEs and see if this theory holds water.

~ Testing the In Between ~

In one NDE,[64] the man describes arriving suddenly in an area that is completely white - white stairs ascending into a white sky with a beautiful white light shining down from above. He describes people standing in a line waiting to ascend the stairs up into the light. At first glance, this sounds like a beautiful, peaceful

---

[64] https://www.nderf.org/Experiences/1salem_nde.html

experience. Yet, the expressions on the faces of those in the line was not one of peace and bliss, but rather distress, fear, and sadness. And then he encountered what he describes as a hideous beast with grizzly-like spiky hair all over its face and large, green, oval-shaped eyes. The creature was angry because the man was holding on to his father, preventing him from climbing the stairs, holding up the line. It growled at him, baring its large white fangs, which struck such fear into the man that he let go.

Obviously, the heavy emotion and intense fear present in this NDE are not at all consistent with pleasant NDEs, despite the beautiful, all-white setting of the scene. But the man wasn't quite tormented by demons the way that others have been. So this NDE falls somewhere in the middle. However, if we think of this NDE from the framework of a cube in the Land Best Forgotten, it might make a little more sense.

Is it not possible that the beautiful all-white environment was simply a projected reality inside his cube? Is it not possible that the father figure and the grizzly beast were demonic visitors playing their part in the scene? Is it not possible that the numerous other people he witnessed standing in a line to ascend the stairs were either apparitions created within the cube or simply other demonic visitors taking the form of human souls? It seems to me that despite the lack of "traditional" forms of demonic torture, this NDE actually makes more sense if the whole thing took place in the virtual reality of a cell in the Land Best Forgotten, possibly accompanied by a few demons to sell the story.

Here[65] we have a man who found himself completely alone, floating on a vast sea, at the mercy of the current. Ahead of him were two large openings, like window panes, each with a different scene beyond. He was pulled through one of those window panes and felt surprised to find himself in a cemetery, completely isolated and alone.

Nothing in this experience matches the patterns found in pleasant NDEs, but then again there is no demonic torture, no moments of terror, and it certainly didn't take place in an empty void. But what if this entire experience actually took place in a cell in the Land Best Forgotten?

Could his cell not appear to be a vast sea? Could it not project the perceived reality of floating through a window into a cemetery? Might that explain why he didn't encounter the Being of light or anyone else during his experience? It seems to me that he was every bit as alone and isolated as those in the void because he was similarly confined to a cubic cell in the Land Best Forgotten, and this surreal environment was merely created by the cell walls.

At first I was unsure about this one[66] because the survivor reports such a peaceful experience in the white space, but a number of elements lead me to believe that this actually took place in a cell in the Land Best Forgotten. First, she describes the environment as "nothingness," but clearly identifies it as a "room" without walls or windows. This sense of being confined to a room with walls you cannot see is exactly the state of those in the cubic cells described by Bryan, and this is remarkably similar

---

[65] https://www.nderf.org/Experiences/1beh_e_probable_nde.html

[66] https://www.nderf.org/Experiences/1blanca_a_nde.html

to the description given by the woman in the 150-foot flames. Also, the NDEr's uncle appears exactly as she remembered him at the end of his life, complete with a walking stick. But in typical pleasant NDEs, people describe their loved ones as being in the prime of their lives - not old and in need of a walking stick.

So then, is it possible that her entire experience actually took place inside a cell? Could it be that the uncle was actually a demonic visitor playing a role to sell the story? After all, Bryan encountered demonic visitors who posed as loved ones and showered him with greetings and affection, so it seems plausible to me that the uncle in this story falls into the same category.

In another NDE[67] we find a man who spent the first part of his journey floating around the scene of his death, visiting the homes of his loved ones, and even traveling into the upper atmosphere where he had an aerial view of the Earth. But then suddenly, all he could see was pitch black. In the void, he experienced flashes of his life, some of which left him feeling deeply guilty and sorrowful. Suddenly, he found himself in a beautiful green meadow, where he entered a house and discovered his father and grandfather - both of whom greeted him with love and affection. They praised him for being a good man and urged him to ensure that his daughter would never lose her religion. As they walked towards a mosque, he stopped and then suddenly found himself back in his body.

At first glance, this NDE seems very pleasant - so much so that, prior to reading Bryan's book, I was convinced that it fell within the realm of pleasant NDEs. But when I revisited this

---

[67] https://www.nderf.org/Experiences/1halil_t_nde.html

account in the early stages of evaluating this framework, there was one reported detail that changed my mind. Read it for yourself, and then answer me this: What is it that happened between his aerial view of the Earth and the meadow where he met his father and grandfather? It went completely black - instantly. He was in the void!

Is it possible, then, that his NDE began with a free exploration around the Earth and up into the atmosphere, but at that very moment, he arrived in his cell? After all, his subsequent life review invoked feelings of guilt and shame - not at all what pleasant NDE accounts describe in the presence of the Being of light. If this is true and he was indeed in a cell, wouldn't that explain the discontinuous and instantaneous changes in scenery? And wouldn't it be possible that the father and grandfather were actually demonic creatures in disguise? It seems to me that, despite its overall pleasant experience, everything after the moment of arrival in the void actually took place in a cell in the Land Best Forgotten.

I found this particular NDE[68] to be very interesting because on the surface it seems so peaceful and beautiful. But if you look a little closer, I think it might be more in line with the idea of confinement in a cubic cell than in the realm of pleasant NDEs. The journey begins with a celestial tour, but then the scene immediately changes without explanation, and then the woman is literally locked in a garden, all alone. And before the guide simply disappears, he says that she must remain captive there until the final day of judgment, despite her angry protest. She

---

[68] https://www.nderf.org/Experiences/1fatma_a_possible_nde.html

tours this vast palatial complex without meeting a single person. The only things she communicates with are a bird and a tree - reminiscent of Bryan's account of demons playing roles of animals and trees in the cell. Though the garden and palace may have seemed beautiful and peaceful, is it not possible that she was not imprisoned in a palace garden, but in a cell in the Land Best Forgotten? I've never heard of a pleasant NDEr in the presence of the Being of light being forcibly confined within a gated wall, but it seems to me that the cubes in the Land Best Forgotten could certainly present that perceived reality.

In yet another NDE,[69] a man encounters what he calls a "blue fairy" who takes him on a journey and leaves him in a "room with cloud walls." At the mere thought of a place to sit, a bench suddenly materializes, and a short time later, three beings emerge from a doorway that appears out of nowhere, including a small, giddy girl. As his experience progresses, the scenery changes from the cloud room to a grassy field on a sunny day, to a small white room, to a cold, damp cave, to a platform in outer space. He interacts with several people who play tricks on him, such as giving him horribly tasting food and drink and then laughing at his disgust. And he describes how the beings are clearly some sort of jackal-faced creatures who wear masks to disguise their true appearance. As the imagery turns darker and the experience more frightening, he hears a voice urging him to pray to Jesus and ask for salvation. He then sees a "man sitting in a giant stone chair" whom he believes to be Jesus, flanked by a silver-winged angel, the Virgin Mary, and an old man whom he believes to be some sort of

---

[69] https://www.nderf.org/Experiences/1jeffrey_c_nde_8024.html

apostle. The giddy girl from earlier quickly sweeps him away into a room with a model of the universe where she explains that souls in heaven are just as troubled as those on Earth and they plead to be sent to material worlds to educate themselves and improve their status in heaven. Jesus and Mary proceed to get angry when he questions their authority, and he is ordered to crawl on the floor and kiss the feet of Jesus - dirty, worn feet with "yellow split toenails."

Let's start with the room that had walls made of clouds where a bench simply materialized and a door appeared out of nowhere. Does this not sound like what one would expect to find in an artificial reality of a cube in the Land Best Forgotten, where the scenery changes instantly and demonic visitors can enter and exit at any time, playing any role they desire in the storyline of the scene? And the people who gave him foul tasting food and drink and then laughed at his disgust - does that not sound like the kind of sick joke demonic beings would enjoy playing on helpless, naive human souls? Even their appearance seemed to be deceptive, as the NDEr reports that they wore masks to hide their true faces. Finally, picture the domineering, judgmental, indignant, and disappointed Jesus character portrayed in the experience as he forces the NDEr to crawl across the floor and kiss dirty, disgusting, yellow toenails. Does this not sound like another sick joke by a demon in role-play? Can you not hear the muffled cackle under its breath as it watches this poor young man suffer through the disgust of kissing these horrendous feet? It seems to me that everything about this experience points to being locked inside a cell in the Land Best Forgotten, visited by several demons playing a role to sell the story.

~ My Conclusion ~

You are, of course, free to draw your own conclusions from the evidence discussed in this chapter. However, when I see the common themes of the mode and direction of travel to the NDE, the swirling earthen-colored vortex, the discontinuous changes of scenery, the interaction with few, if any, characters in the experience, and the emotions of fear, anger, or sadness, it seems to me that such an NDE actually occurred in a cubic cell in the Land Best Forgotten. Is it possible, then, that Bryan's account describes the state of the afterlife for millions, perhaps even billions, of deceased people currently residing in the Land Best Forgotten?

Is it possible that during a distressing NDE, the NDEr is transported to the Land Best Forgotten and placed into their own cubic cell? And that the experience after that point is merely a glimpse of what an afterlife in that facility might look like, before they are returned to the land of the living? Are DNDEs vast and varied, because each one occurs in the subjective reality of a cubic cell, isolated from every other ongoing experience? Could it be that some people remain alone, uninterrupted and untouched by demonic visitors, resulting in a void-type NDE, or perhaps a different experience of complete isolation and loneliness? And that some people encounter demonic visitors in their cube, playing the roles of terrifying creatures, but also of unimposing or even loving characters?

In addition, is it possible that Bryan's account further highlights for us the distinct dichotomy between the location of pleasant NDEs with the Being of light, and the location of distressing NDEs in the Land Best Forgotten? It seems to me that Bryan started with a pleasant NDE, in which he floated up into the dark tunnel and met the Being of light. And it was the swirling vortex that then took him to a completely different realm, namely the Land Best Forgotten, where his distressing NDE began. Then, at the end of his DNDE, the Being of light retrieved him from the Land Best Forgotten and brought him back through the vortex, not to his body, but rather to the place where they first met. A place of spiritual freedom.

As with Bryan, in most pleasant NDEs, the return to the body is continuous. That is to say, they travel back through the tunnel, back to the surface of the Earth, and back to their body. But, just as some DNDErs appear instantly in the cube, many DNDErs don't travel continuously back to their bodies, but rather return instantly at the moment of their resuscitation. Is it possible that this difference is due to the spiritual confinement of the Land Best Forgotten, as opposed to the spiritual freedom in the realm of pleasant NDEs?

In the state of spiritual freedom, perhaps NDErs are free to travel through space and return to their bodies without a discontinuous jump in location. But in the state of spiritual confinement, it seems that the NDErs are trapped in the cubic cell, and can only depart the facility in a manner similar to their arrival, such as a swirling vortex, a black pit, or instantaneous transport.

Therefore, in light of all of the evidence discussed so far, I have come to the following conclusion. This is the framework through which I now view every NDE account:

It seems to me that every NDE occurs either in a state of spiritual freedom with the Being of light, or in a state of spiritual confinement in the Land Best Forgotten.

So now, when I see an NDE that describes elevating upward into a tunnel, an encounter with the Being of light, feelings of *overwhelming* love and compassion like none other experienced in life, and a journey back to the body, it screams spiritual freedom. It seems to me that this person experienced the same spiritual reality described by countless others, a supernatural state in which they were able to interact with the Being of light and other deceased loved ones in a similar situation.

Conversely, when I see an NDE that begins with a descent into a black pit, a void, or a swirling vortex, involves immediate and discontinuous changes of scenery or environment, and ends abruptly, it screams spiritual confinement. It seems to me that this person encountered a unique, individual reality within the confines of a cell in the Land Best Forgotten. Experiences of spiritual confinement can range from isolation in an empty void, to vast open worlds; the person may be utterly alone, or may interact with a small number of demonic creatures role-playing characters in the deceptive reality, or even find themselves face to face with evil, hideous creatures.

Although feelings of fear, terror, anguish, isolation, hopelessness, or despair are excellent indicators of spiritual confinement, I believe some NDEs in spiritual confinement can mimic more pleasant or positive emotions, so I do not always assume that pleasant experiences truly indicate spiritual freedom, especially if the experience contains elements common to others in spiritual confinement. I truly believe that this framework encompasses all near-death experiences, and provides us with a more accurate lens through which to view NDEs.

At this point, I would like to give you the opportunity to pause and investigate some NDE accounts for yourself. However, before I send you off to check my work, I would like to share with you one more NDE story as a word of caution.

> I was pulled out of my body and instantly into a black void. My spirit body was floating in the darkness and it was a lonely place...I knew I was dead and couldn't go back. My thoughts were very fast, like lightning, and my mind was so clear and sharp. My senses were all heightened and my emotions felt more intense. For a long time I was alone in this darkness. Then a speck of light became visible in the distance. I tried to move toward it. It didn't work because I was floating. So then I tried to fly or direct my floating towards the light, but my progress wasn't very good. The light came to me in a zigzag, erratic pattern and at great speed. It was at that moment that I realized the light was a Being. The Being of light was pure white and about 8 to 9 feet tall. I had a peaceful, loving feeling being in this Being's beautiful presence. I believe that Being was an angel. However, I felt like the Being was waiting for something. In my thoughts, I was thinking about how angry I was with God. I was not

repentant for my self-murder. The Being of light left me in a flash. I then felt like a blanket of fear fell on top of me. Never have I felt fear like that, and I have survived a number of murder attempts on my life. The terror gripped me. Then I felt a[n] ice-cold burning sensation, like I was standing on top of Mount Everest. I have always hated the cold and I felt the extremely intense, burning ice. Then I felt big, long needles like the length of a knitting needle but sharp at the tip. The needles were being stabbed into every square inch of my body at the same time. Then the needles were ripped out, all at the same time and then stabbed back in. This was repeated over and over again. It never stopped. I heard screaming and realized it was my scream. I felt like there was a continual pulse of lightning from the tip of my skull to the bottom of my feet. The pain in that place of darkness was worse than anything I had ever felt on earth. It was hundreds or possibly thousands of times worse than what we feel on earth, as the spirit body is so very sensitive. I was thinking about my life and my loved ones and how desperately I wanted for them to avoid this hellish place. I started screaming in my mind, 'I can't take it anymore! I am going crazy in this place let me out!!! Let me out!!!' then I heard what can only be described as demonic laughter that came from a Being right next to me. It was the most evil sound I have ever heard. The darkness was so complete and

I could not see a thing. Then in a flash I was returned to my body.[70]

Obviously, this experience is 100% consistent with the other DNDEs in a state of spiritual confinement in a cubic cell in the Land Best Forgotten. However, did you notice the Being of light she reported right in the middle of the experience? Basking in the warmth of the beautiful Being of light, she said she felt nothing but peace and love. Could this have been the Being of light found in pleasant NDEs, who came to visit her in her cubic cell? There are certainly other NDErs in spiritual confinement who have reported a visit from what seems to be the genuine Being of light.[71] And Bryan reports that the Being of light rescued him from the Land Best Forgotten and brought him back to the realm of pleasant NDEs. So, I suppose it's certainly possible that this is the genuine Being of light.

But in this particular instance, the fact that *this* Being of light instantly disappeared and apparently didn't frighten the demonic creatures away, as Bryan reported in his account, leads me to believe that this Being of light was actually another demonic creature in disguise. If they can appear in a myriad of different forms, couldn't they resemble the Being of light described in pleasant NDEs? And if Bryan's impersonated loved ones could shower him with joy and affection in his DNDE, is it not possible that these creatures could evoke a similar feeling of love in any person confined in a cell?

---

[70] https://www.nderf.org/Experiences/1katrina_nde.html
[71] https://youtu.be/GVMii_SdDwQ?si=rUbtK2uzzkcDEVA4

So it seems to me that we can't rely on the mere presence of the Being of light, or the emotional sensations of peace and love, to rule out an NDE in spiritual confinement, since it is possible that these demonic creatures are impersonating the Being of light in yet another instance of deception. Therefore, if an NDE contains other elements that are more consistent with spiritual confinement, we should allow those elements to weigh more heavily than the seemingly-pleasant emotions of the experience. After all, even in life, the enchanting love-bombing of an abuser can feel genuine, even if the motive behind it is sinister or nefarious. So, please keep that in mind.

With that out of the way, please, take a break and go explore NDE accounts for yourself. Go to the NDERF or IANDS websites. Search YouTube for NDE accounts. Read these experiences, listen to people tell their story, and see for yourself how well this framework fits the evidence. Look for the common elements and patterns that helped build this framework, and see for yourself how well they all fit together. Do this while the framework is fresh in your mind, then come back and we'll dig deeper into the discussion.

6

WHY IT'S TRUE

Though I imagine most of my generation would associate Joe Pesci with his Wet Bandit role in the Home Alone series, for me, the iconic role his name brings to mind (besides Goodfellas, of course) is Vincent Gambini in the film, My Cousin Vinny.

~ SPOILER ALERT ~

In the movie, Ralph Macchio, famous for his role as the Karate Kid, and his best friend, played by Mitchell Whitfield, find themselves wrongly accused of murdering a convenience store clerk in small-town Alabama. They have no hope and no one to call to help them out - except their cousin, Vinny, a struggling New York lawyer. Seen by the locals as yankee outsiders, the trio of New Yorkers are presumed guilty and incompetent before the trial even begins.

The favored town prosecutor builds a fantastic case against the two men, presenting eyewitness testimony that they entered the store, and emerged shortly after the sound of a gunshot. He subpoenas an automotive expert to analyze the rubber on the men's car tires, confirming it perfectly matches the samples taken from the skid marks where the car peeled off in the escape. The wheelbase of the skid marks also aligns perfectly with the car the men were driving. The case appears to be open and shut with no hope for the leading men.

And in what most in the courtroom consider a ridiculous and irrelevant move, Vinny calls his fiancée, Lisa, played by Marisa Tomei, to the stand. What business did she have interfering in this case? She wasn't an eyewitness, she's not an automotive engineer or a chemical specialist, she's not a professional mechanic, she has no expertise in ballistics or other forensic tools that could make a meaningful contribution to the ongoing investigation. And yet, despite her lack of training, despite her professional irrelevance as a hairdresser, it is *her* testimony that wins the case for the defense. How so?

Despite her lack of professional training or certification, Lisa grew up in a family of mechanics and spent most of her childhood working as a mechanic in her father's shop. Through this practical, hands-on experience, she had acquired a considerable amount of general automotive knowledge. It was this knowledge that allowed her to look at the crime scene photos and see something new, something that no one else, not even the experts, had seen. And when she pointed out this powerful and indisputable detail, the experts in the room had no choice but to follow her proposed narrative to its logical conclusion, resulting not only in the acquittal of the defendants, but also in the discovery of the actual killers, with the murder weapon still in their possession.

~ End of Spoilers ~

Likewise, some may question my own lack of expertise on the subject and wonder why anyone should even listen to the framework I'm proposing. I'm not a scholar, I don't have a graduate degree in near-death experiences or other medically related fields. I'm not an expert on death or what comes after death. But, like Lisa, I have acquired a diverse general knowledge in various fields of study, and it is this combination of general knowledge that I believe has led me down a path to formulate this framework and put it all out there for your own evaluation. Like Lisa, I believe I just happened to be in the right place at the right time with the right background to see something that others may have missed.

So in this chapter, I'm going to share with you some of the additional background information that differentiates my perspective and makes my analysis unique. I believe there are certain details that are either ignored or overlooked by many NDE researchers, and it is only when we actually take these factors into account that we can establish a truly coherent and comprehensive framework like the one I have proposed here. These are the reasons why I truly believe that this framework corresponds to reality.

~ Explanatory Power & Scope ~

If you've returned to continue reading this book, I can only assume it's because your NDE investigation has come back consistent with the framework established in the previous chapter. If the opposite were true, I imagine you would simply disregard this entire book and move on with your life. But if you're like me, then it has now become impossible for you to see NDEs in any other light. I suspect that you have found quite a few instances where you could clearly tell whether an NDE occurred in spiritual freedom or confinement, whether due to the direction or means of travel, the appearance of the surroundings, discontinuous changes of scenery, or any number of other details we have discussed so far. The fact that so many NDEs share these common characteristics, regardless of the survivor's race, nationality, or worldview, gives me confidence in the truth of the framework. It truly has the explanatory power and scope to address nearly every NDE I've ever encountered, and it allows us to accept the validity of each experience individually without overlooking the glaring inconsistencies or contradictions between some of them.

Although there will undoubtedly be some NDEs that do not provide enough context to place them firmly in one of the two dichotomous realms, such cases do not undermine the framework because they do not contradict it in any way - they just leave us guessing. I believe we can have confidence in the framework without needing to have 100% certainty about the location of every experience. The fact that it fits the vast majority of NDEs makes the framework a very strong inference.

~ PREDICTIONS ~

Now we come to what I think is often overlooked by professional researchers. And if I'm being honest, I understand why. In fact, I can tell you right now that you may not like this at all. What I'm about to suggest may contradict central tenets of your worldview; it may evoke feelings of disgust or denial; it may even cause you to stop reading this book altogether.

But I hope you will resist those urges. I hope that you have come to see this framework as valid and comprehensive. And I hope you can trust that I've put as much research into what comes next as I have into everything we've covered so far. Just listen to the argument presented in this chapter before you dismiss it. If you don't find it convincing, by all means close the book and get on with your life. But if you *do* decide to go that route, I hope you will at least respect the fact that thousands, if not millions, of people have had near-death experiences, both pleasant and distressing, and it is my sincere desire that no one ever finds their after-death experience comparable to the horror revealed in The Land Best Forgotten. I encourage you to create your own framework and test its explanatory power and scope against what I've presented here. This is too important to just ignore and walk away.

So what is this big, groundbreaking thing? Are you ready for it? Beyond the incredible explanatory power and scope of this framework to address the vast majority of NDEs, I believe this framework is true because Christianity is true, and the predictions Christianity has been making for thousands of years about our existence immediately after death are exactly what we observe through NDEs.

Please don't stop reading yet! Obviously, I'm not going to ask you to simply accept this statement as undeniably true without any proof or justification. So if you're willing to stick around for a few more pages, I'm going to offer you the reasoning behind these statements and leave it up to you to decide whether or not you agree with me. We'll start with why Christianity is true, and then cover some of its relevant predictions.

But before we get into that, I need you to clear your mind of everything you think you know about Christianity and the Christian version of an afterlife (this includes Christians reading this book as well). Despite its prevalent tradition, nowhere does the Bible describe our state after death as a hazy party in the clouds with white-robed, winged versions of our friends and family, doing nothing but sitting around all day playing harps. Nor does the Bible paint a picture of Dante's Inferno or little red devils in tights holding pitchforks. These are mere comic caricatures, and they actually tend to mislead NDE survivors, since what they experienced was completely out of line with these preconceived expectations. If we are to propose a serious answer to the question of why there are both pleasant and distressing NDEs and what they mean, we must make an honest assessment of the actual truth claims of the Christian worldview. So take a moment to prepare your mind for that exploration.

Also, as will probably soon become apparent, much of my theology and Biblical study has been influenced by scholars such as N.T. Wright, Timothy Mackie, and Michael Heiser. These scholars represent a fairly recent movement among Christian theologians to return to the spiritual worldview of the Hebrew authors at the time the Bible was written in order to better understand some of the less concrete details about some of God's other creations in the spiritual or unseen realm. For the sake of time, and to spare you the considerable amount of theological discussion on such topics, I will not delve deeply into the supporting arguments for this particular exegetical framework. If you want to explore it for yourself, I recommend starting with Heiser's book, *The Unseen Realm*. I'm only warning you about this up front because even those who are familiar with the Bible, even many Christians, may find some of what follows in the next few chapters to be a bit new or unfamiliar. So, for your own benefit, we'll wade into that slowly.

~ CHRISTIANITY IS TRUE ~

If you asked 1,000 different Christians why they believe Christianity is true, you'd probably get 1,000 different answers. For some, it's about feelings; for others, perhaps an anecdotal experience has brought them to that conclusion. As an engineer and one who spends more time in the intellectual side of my mind than the emotional side, my belief in the truth of Christianity is evidential in nature. Whether it's the philosophical logical arguments or the myriad of historical and archaeological discoveries, I have spent a considerable amount of time over the last 10 years familiarizing myself with the logical and intellectual reasons to believe that Christianity is true.

And yet I find so many of these arguments too abstract and open to interpretation. I find them too intellectual for most everyday conversation, and they rely on knowledge or presupposed knowledge of abstract concepts like "before the big bang" or a standard definition of "objective morality". However, I think there is an argument that is a little more accessible to most people. I guess you could say it's my favorite argument, and probably one of the main reasons I remain a Christian in an increasingly post-Christian culture.

Historian, New Testament scholar, and theologian Gary Habermas has devoted much of his professional study to what is known as the "historical Jesus" - essentially, the Jesus that we can find attested through historical documentation, including extra-biblical sources, rather than simply through the dogmatic teachings of the Christian church. One of his greatest contributions in this area is the formulation of what he calls the "minimal facts argument for the resurrection of Jesus." The core premise of the argument is that there are a small number of historical facts that are agreed upon by historical scholars, both Christian and non-Christian alike, which build a cumulative case for the truth of Jesus' life, death, and bodily resurrection nearly 2,000 years ago. Here is a brief summary to get us started.

As agnostic New Testament scholar Bart Ehrman states, "The view that Jesus existed is held by virtually every expert on the planet."[72] Atheist New Testament scholar Gerd Ludemann goes on to say, "Jesus' death as a consequence of crucifixion is indisputable."[73] Habermas notes that at least 75% of

---

[72] Ehrman, Bart D. Did Jesus Exist?: The Historical Argument for Jesus of Nazareth. New York: HarperOne, 2012. 4.
[73] Ludemann, Gerd. The Resurrection of Christ: A Historical Inquiry. 2004. 50

non-Christian scholars agree that Jesus' tomb was found empty,[74] and as D.H. van Daalen says, "It is extremely difficult to object to the empty tomb on historical grounds; those who deny it do so on the basis of theological or philosophical assumptions."[75] Ludemann goes on to say, "It may be taken as historically certain that Peter and the disciples had experiences after Jesus' death in which Jesus appeared to them as the risen Christ."[76] And Habermas further points out that even non-Christian scholars generally agree that both Paul, the former persecutor and murderer of Christians, and James, the skeptical brother of Jesus, both converted to Christianity and became early leaders in the Christian church.[77]

These simple historical facts - Jesus' life and death by crucifixion, the empty tomb, the post-mortem appearances of Jesus to many witnesses, and the conversion of James and Paul - demand an explanation. These facts are accepted even by non-Christian scholars because the historical evidence, including sources outside the Bible itself, is simply too strong to deny them. Together, they form a comprehensive set of data that must be accounted for by any worldview, religious or otherwise. And it is Habermas' contention that these facts are best explained by the genuine historicity of the bodily resurrection of Jesus.

[74] Gary Habermas. "Resurrection Research from 1975 to the Present: What are Critical Scholars Saying". Journal for the Study of the Historical Jesus, 3.2 (2005), pp. 135-153
[75] D. H. van Daalen, The Real Resurrection (London: Collins, 1972) 41
[76] Gerd Ludemann, What Really Happened to Jesus?, trans. John Bowden (Louisville, Kent.: Westminster John Knox Press, 1995), p. 80
[77] Gary R. Habermas. Dialog: A Journal of Theology, Vol. 45; No. 3 (Fall, 2006), pp. 288-297

The argument is admittedly an inference to the "best explanation" given the evidence, so of course, it has not gone unchallenged. Some have claimed that Jesus was never buried in a tomb, but was placed in an open grave and his body was eaten by wild animals, affording early Christians the opportunity to claim that Jesus had risen from the dead, left his tomb, and then ascended into Heaven. Others have claimed that the body was stolen from the tomb, most likely by Jesus' followers, who then fabricated outlandish claims about His resurrection and ascension. There even exists a theory that Jesus wasn't really dead at all, that he merely rested and recuperated in the tomb, and then escaped into hiding where he continued to heal. Still others claim that Jesus' followers hallucinated due to the intense grief of losing their friend and teacher. And many of these hypotheses hinge on the theory that some sort of "impostor Jesus" appeared to the disciples and other early Jewish converts, and somehow played the role so convincingly that the early Jewish followers were duped into building an entire religion around this impeccable charlatan. But let's take a few minutes to apply some critical thinking to these objections.

First, the authors of the Biblical gospels identified by name the owner of the tomb in which they claimed Jesus was buried - Joseph of Arimathea, a member of the Jewish Sanhedrin. Yet neither Joseph nor his fellow members of the Sanhedrin denied this claim. If anyone would have seized the opportunity to deny Jesus' burial in a tomb and offer up an alternative narrative, it would have been these men. Yet none of them did. Similarly, the Romans never denied the Biblical claim that the tomb was closed and sealed with a Roman insignia. Again, if they wanted to crush the early Christian narrative of an empty tomb, a complete denial of the existence of said tomb would have weighed heavily in their favor. But, as with the Sanhedrin, this argument was never utilized. Together, these two prominent groups of non-Christians provide us with a hostile witness testimony to the fact that Jesus was indeed buried in a tomb and not in an open grave.

As for the stolen body, we can say with certainty that neither the Jews nor the Romans would have stolen it. Had the body been in their possession when Christians began to create a stir in the city with their claims of a risen Messiah, they could have immediately quashed those claims by presenting the body for public display. But, that did not happen. They didn't even try to claim that they had taken it but subsequently lost it. So we can safely conclude that neither the Romans or the Jews had possession of the body, leaving only the apostles, who would have had to overcome some pretty serious obstacles to get the body into their possession.

Their first obstacle would have been the Roman soldiers standing guard outside the tomb. These soldiers had been ordered to guard the tomb, knowing full well that disobedience could easily have resulted in dismissal, severe beatings, or possibly even death. Are we really to believe that a small, impoverished band of tradesmen, fearing for their lives after their leader had just been executed, would have the might to overpower them, or the financial means to bribe them? That's a pretty hard pill to swallow.

But even if they could get past the soldiers themselves, the next obstacle would be the tomb, which was covered by a massive stone. In and of itself, the stone might not have been a problem for a large enough group, but the real problem is that the tomb was sealed with a Roman insignia. Therefore, it was against Roman law to break the seal and open the tomb. Would this small group of men really have the courage to break that seal, thereby sentencing themselves to an execution similar to that which Jesus had just received? And if they did break the seal, why didn't Rome ever charge or prosecute them for such a crime? The fact that they were never charged with the crime of breaking the seal only makes sense if the Romans themselves knew for a fact that it wasn't Jesus' followers who broke the seal and opened the tomb.

Finally, keep in mind that Jesus died on the Jewish Passover, which meant that countless Jews from all around Judea would have made the pilgrimage to Jerusalem for the event, and many would not have had a home to stay in. So the hillsides would have been lined with campsites, every room in the city would have been occupied and overflowing, and the streets would have been filled to the brim with people. So even if the apostles were able to bypass the guards, even if they had broken the Roman seal (without ever being charged with a crime against Rome for doing so), and even if they had been able to move the stone, they would still have had to remove the body from the tomb and get it out of the city to a disposal site without being seen by the thousands of people lining the streets and countryside. It would only take one witness to describe the clandestine operation and reveal the chosen disposal site to unravel the entire ruse like a ball of yarn. And yet, not a single person in the entire city ever claimed to have witnessed such an audacious stunt, and neither Jewish or Roman authorities ever attempted to do so much as fabricate such a false-witness. So, under closer scrutiny, the theory of a stolen body doesn't exactly hold water, and if we choose to stand on it, we can only do so without any historical reason or evidence to support our philosophical presupposition.

In my personal opinion, the theory that Jesus wasn't really dead is nothing more than grasping at straws. Not only does it contradict every historical source we have on the subject, even those outside the Bible, it also sells the Romans short. They were masters of death, constantly devising more cruel and entertaining forms of execution. To think that the Romans were fooled into believing that Jesus was dead when he actually wasn't is just not consistent with everything we know about the Romans. Furthermore, I doubt if anyone would have believed Jesus' claims of divinity if he had merely escaped a failed execution attempt, but still needed time to slowly heal and recover like any other normal human being. So I really have trouble lending credence to this unsubstantiated and unattested theory.

Although the hallucination theory looks good at first glance, it has some pretty big holes that need to be filled. For example, the Bible claims that not only did the apostles see Jesus, but also hundreds of others in and around Jerusalem. Yet, there has never been a documented case or evidence of a group hallucination where so many people hallucinated the same thing. Moreover, if grief was the catalyst for the apostles' hallucinations, as some have suggested, why would Paul have seen Jesus as well? Paul was a Jewish Pharisee, the very group of Jewish leaders who wanted to see Jesus dead. He even admits to persecuting Christians, imprisoning them, and condoning their execution. For Paul, grieving the death of Jesus wouldn't have even entered the picture. So it seems to me that the hallucination theory not only lacks historical support, but also flies in the face of everything we know about hallucinations and the mechanisms that cause them.

Similarly, the impostor theory makes no sense in light of the conversions of James and Paul. Why would Paul believe a guy who claims to be Jesus but offers no supernatural proof of that claim? Even if he couldn't explain the empty tomb, the jump from, "So you say you are this guy who died" to "You're the Lord of the universe, for whom I will gladly give up everything, including my life" is quite extraordinary, and I think such a claim would have required more extraordinary evidence to back it up than any human being could offer. Paul gave up a life of power, respect, and status in the Jewish community, only to spend the last 30 years of his life suffering persecution and even execution for his refusal to deny the divinity of Jesus. Those are some incredibly high stakes, and tremendously significant sacrifices, and I just have a hard time seeing how any mere human could convince Paul to make that transition.

Likewise, James was Jesus' brother. Can we honestly believe that James wouldn't be able to spot the impostor or disprove him by questioning him on some obscure childhood memory? In his letter to the tribes of Israel, James identifies himself as a bond-servant of Jesus - his older brother. So this impostor must have been so persuasive that he not only convinced James of his false identity, but also convinced him to subjugate himself, devoting his entire life to his older brother as Lord and master of the universe. That's a tough pill to swallow for any younger brother, let alone one who didn't believe in Jesus' claims while he was alive. James likely witnessed Jesus vomiting as a child, and probably wrestled with him on the nearby hillsides. It seems to me that the evidence required to justify a conversion from that perspective to one of servitude, even to the point of losing his life for refusing to deny the divinity of his brother, would be far greater than any mere impostor could manifest.

Nevertheless, many claim that Occam's Razor justifies these alternative theories because Jesus' resurrection is only possible if God exists, and to posit the existence of a God just to support a resurrection hypothesis is too ad hoc. Many assume that God does not exist, so the least ad hoc position is to embrace one or more of these alternative theories to explain the historical facts outlined in Habermas' argument above. But given the evidence we have uncovered through the NDE research outlined in this book, is belief in a God really unfounded?

Thousands of near-death experiences, from people of every race, religion and worldview, from every nation around the globe, reveal a Being of light that is loving and compassionate, quick to forgive, and gracious in the face of embarrassing or shameful moments revealed in their life reviews. It cares deeply for every person It meets, It knows everything about them, and has not only seen their entire lives, but also felt the impact that each moment has had on others. By offering NDErs the chance to remain in the spiritual realm or return to their physical bodies, It has demonstrated, countless times, Its absolute power over everything, even life and death. It seems to reside in a spiritual reality beyond our material universe yet seems to be able to observe and interact with things within it. If this isn't the definition of an all-knowing, all-seeing, all-powerful, all-loving, ever-present, transcendent Being, the typical attributes we associate with "God," then I don't know what is.

There may be many who would associate this God-like character from NDEs with deities other than the God of the Bible. And that's fine, if that's where they truly believe the evidence has led them. However, it should be abundantly clear that NDEs give us compelling reasons to believe in the existence of at least some sort of God-like Being with absolute power over life and death.

In that case, is it really a stretch of the imagination to believe that this God could have sent Jesus back to life, just as we have witnessed in thousands of NDE accounts from all around the world? If we can accept thousands of stories from NDErs over the last 50 years that detail an encounter with a loving, personal God who sent them back to life after they had died, do we have any logical basis for ardently rejecting the *possibility* that the same thing happened to Jesus 2,000 years ago? I would argue that the transcendent view of NDEs, the acceptance of these accounts as genuine out-of-body experiences, and the subsequent return to life in the material body make it almost impossible to reject, a priori, the claim that Jesus rose from the dead. And if that did indeed happen, if Jesus was indeed sent back to continue living, then isn't the resurrection of Jesus the simplest explanation for the empty tomb, the absence of Jesus' dead body, the post-mortem appearances, and the conversions of James and Paul?

NDEs give us ample reason to believe that God exists, and they give us significant evidence for the possibility of human resurrection from the dead, including the resurrection of Jesus.

Therefore, thanks to the evidence from NDEs, it seems to me that the primary objection to Habermas' argument is nullified, and the least ad hoc position must now be the simple, straightforward interpretation of the Biblical claim - Jesus was raised from the dead. And if God exists, and Jesus was raised from the dead, then the best explanation of these two facts can only be the truth of the Christian worldview.

~ BIBLICAL PREDICTIONS ~

So far, we've seen that NDEs provide us with very good reasons to believe in the existence of an all-knowing, all-loving, ever-present, spiritual Being who can interact with our material universe and has control over life and death itself. And that the existence of this Being, attested by thousands of eyewitness testimonies from NDErs, gives us significantly more confidence in the resurrection of Jesus as the best explanation of the historical facts highlighted by Habermas. The Bible has been standing on the truth of these two claims for thousands of years. So then, might it be worth your time to explore what else the Bible has to say about life and death? Does the Christian concept of our existence immediately after death correspond with the NDE evidence from which we have built the framework? Does the Bible contradict what we observe in NDEs, or does it offer more context and clarity to the accounts from thousands of NDE survivors from all around the world?

Before we explore the answer to this question, I would like to address what many Christians consider to be an obstacle to further investigation of NDE evidence, namely Hebrews 9:27, where the author clearly states that all men are destined to die but once and then face judgment. For many Christians, this single verse precludes even the possibility that NDEs are objective encounters with an immaterial afterlife, because if the survivors were truly dead, they would have stayed dead and faced judgment. In response to this objection, I would simply point out that the Bible specifically mentions 9 instances beyond Jesus' own resurrection in which the dead were brought back to life: 1 Kings 17; 2 Kings 4:13; Luke 7:8; John 11, Matthew 27, Acts 9:20.

In the Luke 8 passage, when Jesus Himself brings back to life Jarius' daughter, the mourners in the crowded house mocked Jesus for claiming that she was only sleeping and wasn't really dead, because they all knew the difference between sleep and death. Despite her clinical death, Jesus viewed her situation with a more nuanced perspective than the bystanders in the room.

Or consider Lazarus as described in John 11. Jesus clearly states that Lazarus' sickness will not end in death (v4), but then just a few verses later, Jesus clearly states that Lazarus had died (v14). And yet, after four days in the tomb, clearly dead and not just sleeping, Lazarus was brought back to life. Was Jesus lying in verse four? Or did He not know what would happen to Lazarus? For anyone who believes in the divinity of Jesus, the answer to both of these questions must be "no." If we are to believe that both of Jesus' statements are completely true, then there must be more nuance to Jesus' perspective on death than we might perceive through our limited earthly lens.

Could we not apply the same nuance to more modern instances of death and resuscitation? If God has complete power over life and death, if He has clearly demonstrated His ability to bring people back to life, then on what Biblical grounds can we declare such an act impossible today? If Jesus demonstrated a nuanced distinction between the condition of someone who is clinically dead but who can still come back to life (John 11:14) and someone who will remain in the grave forever (John 11:4), on what Biblical grounds do we deny that same nuanced perspective from informing the message of Hebrews 9:27? If God knows that someone who is clinically dead will not remain in the grave, if He has the ultimate authority over our eternal destiny in the afterlife, on what Biblical grounds can we prevent God from giving someone a small preview of what the afterlife might be like before He brings them back to life?

I raise this point because I believe it's important not to let an eisegetical imposition of our modern concept of "death" on Hebrews 9:27 keep Christians from exploring what the Bible actually says about our state immediately after death. As I'll explain here, there is actually a very strong correlation between the Bible's teachings on the afterlife and what we discover in NDE accounts. So again, I want to urge you to put aside any preconceived notions or images you may have about the Biblical concept of life after death, and simply let the text speak for itself. This is going to be pretty Biblically heavy, so take your time and ensure you get a solid grasp of what I'm going to cover here. Let's dig in.

~ THE BEING OF LIGHT ~

The first Biblical narrative of interest is what is known as the Transfiguration of Jesus, in which Peter, James, and John were given a glimpse of Jesus' true, glorious form. Matthew (v 17:2) describes Jesus' face with the Greek word *lampo*, which means to shine or radiate light. Mark (v 9:3) describes Jesus' clothing with the Greek word *stilbo*, meaning to gleam, flash or glisten. And Luke (v 9:29) describes Jesus' garments with the Greek word *exastrapto*, which means to send forth or radiate light. Although many Christians debate exactly what happened at the Transfiguration, it should be unequivocally clear that the authors of the three synoptic gospels were trying to describe Jesus' appearance as radiating an immense light. It's certainly circumstantial, but given the strong correlation between the Being of light in NDEs and the person of Jesus, it seems to me that this Biblical description of Jesus in His true, glorious form is so much more than a mere coincidence. I believe that this represents a 2,000 year old written account of Jesus seen in the form of the same "Being of light" revealed in modern NDEs.

Even in Acts 9, when Saul is confronted by Jesus, the situation is described as a light shining all around him, not a physical body as in the earlier appearances of Jesus. Again, this is entirely circumstantial and speculative, but it seems to me that after Jesus' ascension (Acts 1), He has taken on His true form, the form previewed at the transfiguration. He now exists as a Being who radiates an immense light, who resides beyond our material observation, yet has the power to make himself known to those whom He chooses. In my opinion, this is only the beginning of the numerous accounts to come detailing an encounter with an all-loving Being of light, and it would make perfect sense that this is the form of Jesus observed by most who now meet Him during a near-death experience.

So when we read George Ritchie's account of the Being of light flooding his small hospital room with light and commanding him, "Stand up. You are in the presence of the Son of God," it makes perfect sense. The Being of light was declaring to George His exact identity, and the identity He was claiming was that of Jesus, the one and only Son of God.

And in Bryan's account, the Being of light instructs him to "say two words at that particular point of overwhelming and they are: My Name in your tongue and my Title." Throughout his time in the Land Best Forgotten, Bryan muttered these two words over and over, rolling off his lips like a machine gun, and it was these two words that kept the evil creatures at bay and prevented them from harming him. What were those two words, that name and title claimed by the Being of light that commanded power and authority even over those evil creatures in that horrible place? *Jesus Christ.*

And these two accounts are certainly not unique. In fact, I invite you to go back to your previous NDE study if you feel the need. Simply note the prevalence of Jesus in so many of these accounts, regardless of the worldview of the NDErs, and note how often the person of Jesus is directly connected to the Being of light revealed in these accounts. As I discussed in the previous chapter, there are certainly instances of other beings of light, and there are even occurrences of other religious figures in some experiences. But when Jesus is mentioned, it is almost always in the form of this loving, forgiving Being of light that so many survivors report.

But this description only pertains to Jesus and how He would appear to those who meet Him today. The Bible also has a significant amount of revelation about what we ourselves can expect to find after we die, and it's nothing like what you learned in Sunday school.

~ THE LAND OF THE DEAD ~

First, let's just rip off the Band-Aid: the Land Best Forgotten is not Hell. Well, at least it's not the "lake of fire" Hell which is to be the final destination for Satan and his followers. Rather, the Land Best Forgotten is a temporary holding facility where the dead await the final resurrection and judgment. More specifically, it is only one of multiple locations within the land of the dead.

In the Tanakh (i.e. the Hebrew Bible, or roughly the Old Testament), we find the Hebrew word *sheol*, which is essentially the land of the dead. Sheol is the place where both the righteous and the wicked go after they die.

> But if the Lord creates something new, and the ground opens its mouth and swallows them up with all that belongs to them, and they go down alive into **Sheol**, then you shall know that these men have despised the Lord." (Numbers 16:30 ESV)

> The wicked shall return to **Sheol**, all the nations that forget God. (Psalm 9:17 ESV)

> Then Jacob tore his garments and put sackcloth on his loins and mourned for his son many days. All his

sons and all his daughters rose up to comfort him, but he refused to be comforted and said, "No, I [Jacob] shall go down to **Sheol** to my son [Joseph], mourning." Thus his father wept for him. (Genesis 37:34-35 ESV)

Sheol from beneath is excited over you to meet you when you come; It arouses for you the spirits of the dead, all the leaders of the earth; It raises all the kings of the nations from their thrones. (Isaiah 14:9)

Notice two immediate points of interest here. First, note that both the wicked nations (Psalm 9) and the righteous Joseph and Jacob (Genesis 37) are said to go to Sheol when they die. Not only does this confirm a continued existence after death, but it ascribes a common destination to all people, regardless of their nationality or standing before God. Second, note the direction of travel is downward. Although circumstantial and based heavily on the prevailing cosmological model at the time, I do find it interesting that the Bible chooses to describe the journey to Sheol as a downward trajectory, given a similar direction of travel to the Land Best Forgotten as revealed in NDEs.

But that's really all we get from the Hebrew Scriptures. There isn't much additional description or context about what Sheol might look like, or what one might expect to experience there. However, the Septuagint, which is roughly a Greek translation of the Hebrew Scriptures, translates the Hebrew word *sheol* into the Greek word *hades*. And in the New Testament, we can find additional elaboration on the nature of Sheol, also called Hades.

> "Finally, the poor man died and was carried by the angels to sit beside Abraham at the heavenly banquet. The rich man also died and was buried, and he went to the place of the dead [**Hades**]. There, in torment, he saw Abraham in the far distance with Lazarus at his side. The rich man shouted, 'Father Abraham, have some pity! Send Lazarus over here to dip the tip of his finger in water and cool my tongue. I am in anguish in these flames.' "But Abraham said to him, 'Son, remember that during your lifetime you had everything you wanted, and Lazarus had nothing. So now he is here being comforted, and you are in anguish. And besides, there is a great chasm separating us. No one can cross over to you from here, and no one can cross over to us from there.' (Luke 16:22-26 NLT)

Notice that, here in Jesus' parable, both the righteous Lazarus and the wicked rich man went to Hades, where Abraham was already waiting, echoing the Jewish concept of Sheol as a land of the dead for both righteous and unrighteous souls. But here, we get additional information about a chasm that separates two very different regions within Sheol. In one region, the righteous man is in fellowship with Abraham, enjoying a great banquet. And in the other region, the wicked man is alone, suffering in torment. The message from Jesus is clear - once a person dies and enters his assigned region, there is no crossing over between them.

But let's pause for a moment and look at the Greek concept of Hades, since Jesus uses this word in a way that is consistent with what was traditionally associated with Sheol. In Greek mythology, Hades is simply the realm of the dead, also known as the underworld, where all people, both good and bad, go after they die. An idea not too far removed from the concept of Sheol that we've discussed so far. But within the realm of Hades, there was a region known as Tartarus, which was said to be a dark and gloomy place where wicked human souls live in torment. Again, somewhat analogous to the part of Sheol where the "rich man" found himself, as described by Jesus above.

However, according to Greek mythology, Tartarus is not only a place of torment for wicked human souls, but also *a dungeon to restrain the Titans*. Therefore, Greek audiences would have viewed the region of Tartarus as a unique location within Hades, where one could find not only wicked human souls, but also more powerful beings, perhaps even those descended from the gods.

Now, I'm not saying that we should base our view of the afterlife on Greek mythology. But rather, I'm just pointing out that the New Testament writers, especially those steeped in Greek and Roman culture, would have been well aware of these cultural beliefs at the time. And that's interesting because Peter, while imprisoned in Rome, wrote a letter to his fellow Christians shortly before his death, in which he tries to encourage the church to remain faithful to the teachings of Jesus, and warns of the judgment that awaits those who spread false doctrines. Of particular interest is 2 Peter 2:4, where he speaks of God's judgment on those angels who rebelled and opposed God's design and beauty, and reminds the church that even those elevated spiritual beings were cast into Hell.

> For if God did not spare **angels** when they sinned, but **cast them into hell** and committed them to chains of gloomy darkness to be kept until the judgment; (2 Peter 2:4 ESV)

But what's unique here is that Peter doesn't use the word *hades* when naming hell, nor does he use *sheol*, nor even *gehenna*, which was a word often used by Jesus himself. Instead, the word he chooses is unique and does not appear anywhere else in the entire Bible, New Testament or Old. The word he uses is *tartaroo*, which has its etymological root in the Greek word *tartarus*.

It seems to me that Peter is tracking with this idea that deep in the pit of Hell, alongside wicked humans who reside in torment, we also find more powerful spiritual beings.

Furthermore, if we look more closely at the idea of the Titans in Greek mythology, it may lead us to another interesting revelation. It may come as a surprise to some that the Bible, at least the Septuagint translation, actually contains the Greek word *titanes*, from which we get the English word "Titans." It appears in 2 Samuel 5:18, and again in verse 22. But why is it there? Is the Bible actually confirming the Greek mythological story of the Titans? Not exactly.

The original Hebrew word which was translated as *titanes* in the Septuagint was *rephaim*, which, when traced through Genesis, Deuteronomy, Joshua, 2 Samuel, 1 Chronicles, and Isaiah, refers to a very ancient race of Canaanite people groups known for their gigantic stature. Think of Og, the king of Bashan, who was said to have a bed more than 13 feet long (Deuteronomy 3:11), or Goliath, the archetype of the giants described in the Bible. These Rephaim were great warriors and kings among the Canaanite peoples, and while perhaps not literally "gigantic" in stature, they were certainly said to be much taller than most people of the time.

Most Biblical scholars believe that the Rephaim were descended from the original "giants" described in the Bible - the Nephilim - on account of Deuteronomy 2:11 and Numbers 13:33, which describe the Anakites as both Nephilim and Rephaim. Genesis 6 describes how the "sons of God," which Heiser contends are powerful spiritual beings created by God and given dominion over earthly nations, saw the beauty of human women and decided to take them for themselves, resulting in the birth of the Nephilim. Whether or not this was a literal sexual relationship is still up for debate, but what's important to note here is the parallel language to the Adam and Eve story in the Garden. Just as Eve saw the apple and desired it, resulting in the "fall" of mankind, so too did these spiritual beings see and desire human women. The implication, according to Heiser and other Biblical scholars, is that this moment describes a time when these powerful spiritual beings, these "sons of God," experienced their own "fall" from grace and chose to rebel against God in their own way.

So the text seems to indicate that these other spiritual beings were somehow able to produce offspring with the human women, and their offspring were called Nephilim. These Nephilim were said to be much larger than the average human of that time in history, as were their descendants, the Rephaim. And because the Nephilim originated in an unsanctioned union between humans and the sons of God, they were distinct from the human lineage descended from Adam. They were something more than human, and so were their descendants, the Rephaim.

Interestingly, however, the term *rephaim* appears in an entirely different context in Hebrew literature, both within and outside of the Biblical canon. In this context, *rephaim* refers to dead spiritual beings who reside in Sheol. And not just any spiritual beings, but specifically spiritual beings who sow seeds of wickedness, and wait at the end of the road for those who do the same.

> So you will be delivered from the forbidden woman, from the adulteress with her smooth words, who forsakes the companion of her youth and forgets the covenant of her God; for her house sinks down to death, and **her paths to the departed [*rephaim*]**; none who go to her come back, nor do they regain the paths of life. (Proverbs 2:16-19 ESV)

> The woman Folly is loud; she is seductive and knows nothing. She sits at the door of her house; she takes a seat on the highest places of the town,

calling to those who pass by, who are going straight on their way, "Whoever is simple, let him turn in here!" And to him who lacks sense she says, "Stolen water is sweet, and bread eaten in secret is pleasant." But he does not know that **the dead [*rephaim*] are there**, that her guests are **in the depths of Sheol**. (Proverbs 9:13-18 ESV)

One who wanders from the way of good sense will rest in **the assembly of the dead [*rephaim*]**. (Proverbs 16:21 ESV)

Thus, in several instances, Proverbs warns that seeking after sins and temptations of this world will result in a departure to Sheol, where the sinner will reside in the presence of this "assembly" of the Rephaim. This concept is reinforced even further by the prophet, Isaiah, when he writes a prophetic message pertaining to the downfall of the king of Babylon.

Sheol beneath is stirred up to meet you when you come; **it rouses the shades [*rephaim*] to greet you**, all who were leaders of the earth; it raises from their thrones **all who were kings of the nations**. (Isaiah 14:9 ESV)

So, in a single sentence, Isaiah claims that these Rephaim, whom he equates with great deceased kings and leaders of nations who now reside in Sheol, are roused to meet the great and evil king of Babylon. But if these Rephaim were confined in chains, or in our case in a cell, they wouldn't be free to greet this king as he descends into Sheol; they wouldn't even be aware of his arrival. Although it's not explicitly stated, the fact that these Rephaim are described as existing in an assembly, as having "thrones" in Sheol, as being roused to greet human souls upon their arrival, all seem to me to indicate that these powerful spiritual beings reside in Sheol, yet have a freedom there that is beyond the restrictions imposed on the human souls. It seems to me that in this realm of torment for the unrighteous, we should expect to find a host of unrighteous spiritual beings, free to roam and "welcome" human arrivals, aware of events happening around them, not confined in a solitary prison cell or in chains.

I believe this makes sense if we go back to the origin of these Rephaim, descendants of the demigod-like "Nephilim." Although these Rephaim were partly human, meaning that their unrighteous soul must go to Hades after death, they were also connected to something more powerful, something potentially created by these spiritual beings called the "sons of God" in Genesis 6. So while they may reside in Sheol, more specifically in the part of Sheol reserved for the unrighteous, they would very likely have more power, authority, and freedom in this spiritual realm than the humans there, as reinforced by the passages cited above. This would perfectly explain the existence of the "demonic" creatures in the Land Best Forgotten, who lived there but could move in and out of the cubes where humans were confined, and who expressed a hatred for God and for the humans He created.

While this is interesting in and of itself, Isaiah goes on just a few verses later to bring to light yet another prediction about the existence of the unrighteous dead in Sheol.

> But you are brought down to **Sheol**, to the **far reaches of the pit**. (Isaiah 14:15 ESV)

There is one detail here that particularly piqued my interest. Isaiah states that Sheol, at least the area for the unrighteous, is a "pit," using the Hebrew word *bor*, which primarily means a pit, well, or cistern. However, of the 30 instances of this word found in the Bible, this is the only verse that refers to the "far reaches" of the pit. In nearly every other instance, the pit is simply something into which someone is dumped or contained, or a hole from which water is drawn. There is not a single mention of "far reaches" elsewhere so I began to wonder why the phrase is there. And here is where I landed.

The Hebrew word here for "far reaches" is *yerekhah*, which refers to territorial boundaries or coastlines, but more often, to the sides of an object. Like the side walls of the tabernacle (Exodus 26:22), or David hiding in a dark corner of the cave when Saul entered (1 Samuel 24:3). So what I see here is a reference to the idea that the evil king's ultimate destination is not just the pit itself, but rather somewhere along the sides of the pit, as if embedded in the walls of the pit itself, rather than simply falling to the bottom. This concept is further reinforced by Ezekiel (v 32:23), who explicitly states that the graves of the evil Assyrian army lie in the *yerekhah bor*, the far reaches or outer side walls of the pit.

So let's summarize the true Biblical teaching on what happens to the souls of the unrighteous immediately after death. They go down to Sheol, a place of torment, a place where they are isolated from the souls of the righteous and where they are prevented from returning to life of their own accord. It describes Sheol as a pit and explains that the final destination for human souls is actually a place along the sides of the pit itself, not simply piled up at the bottom. It predicts the existence of a horde of spiritual beings who reside in this place; powerful, unruly, and malevolent, yet they have a freedom there that is not afforded to the human souls who reside there. These beings are even said to "greet" humans as they arrive at this terrible place, confirming their awareness of human arrival and their ability to interact with humans in any way they choose.

If you've been paying attention, you'll notice that this description perfectly matches Bryan's distressing NDE as he *descended* into the Land Best Forgotten. He described the *pit* bordered by a wide road that spiraled like a staircase. He identified the means of *torment and confinement* as the cubic cells into which each human soul was placed. And he placed the location of these cubes along the *outer perimeter* of the structure, opposite the central hole in the pit. He experienced firsthand the greetings and visitations of *malevolent spiritual beings* who had the power to move in and out of the cubic cells, had full awareness of the life and history of the cell's occupant, and could physically interact with the human prisoners in horrifying ways.

So the Biblical text, written thousands of years ago, perfectly predicts the underlying reality of the land of the dead as revealed to Bryan in his NDE. And since Bryan personally experienced a virtual reality in his own cube, and witnessed numerous other human souls living in their own personal realities in their own cubes, we can come to the point of describing every distressing NDE as occurring in the Land Best Forgotten, also known as Sheol. Distressing NDEs are therefore only a taste of what an existence in Sheol after death might be like, an existence in spiritual confinement within a cell, isolated from other human souls, possibly interacting with other shape-shifting spiritual beings, within a virtual world experience created by the walls of the cubic cell.

We must be careful not to conflate Sheol with Gehenna or the Lake of Fire, which comes into play only after the final judgment of all mankind (Revelation). When we talk about the state immediately after death, we're talking exclusively about Sheol, and the Biblical descriptions of Sheol fit perfectly with the realm of spiritual confinement revealed by NDE evidence.

And I'm not the only one to have discovered this phenomenon. There are numerous DNDE survivors themselves who have returned seeking the best explanation for their experience, and have discovered that explanation within the pages of the Bible. For example, there is a man, a self-proclaimed "anti-theist," who found himself in the void during his NDE. After he returned home and took the time to study the meaning behind his NDE, he found the Biblical concept of Sheol to be the best explanation for his experience, exactly what I'm proposing here, and he subsequently rejected his materialistic, atheistic worldview in favor of one that actually fit the evidence of his NDE - Christianity.[78]

However, we haven't yet addressed the issue of spiritual freedom. The passage from Luke 16 cited above seems to indicate that when a righteous person dies, he or she also descends to Hades, just to a different region. But we have discovered that NDErs travel *upward* to the realm of spiritual freedom, not downward. So does this contradict our framework? According to most Biblical scholars, no, it doesn't, because the righteous souls no longer reside in that region of Hades, but rather are with God in His heavenly kingdom.

~ Paradise ~

> Therefore it says, "When he ascended on high **he led a host of captives**, and he gave gifts to men."
> (Ephesians 4:8 ESV)

Although Paul is referring here to Psalm 68, many believe that the idea of leading a host of captives here refers to Jesus freeing those awaiting in the righteous side of Sheol; that Jesus has essentially carried them with Him to the promised freedom of a life with God. This belief is certainly not uncontested, but even without this particular interpretation of the Pauline verse, there are numerous other verses which reinforce the idea that the righteous are no longer waiting in Sheol.

Jesus himself tells a thief on the cross next to his own that they will be together in Paradise, not Sheol. Here in Luke 23:43,

---

[78] https://www.nderf.org/Experiences/1desmond_h_nde.html

the word for paradise is the same Greek translation for Eden - the place of paradise where God and man dwelt together in perfect fellowship. Furthermore, in Philippians 1:23 and 2 Corinthians 5:8, Paul clearly states that at the time of his death he will "be with Christ," and "at home with the Lord." Obviously, going to be with Jesus requires that we travel to His current location. But where is that? It's *above*, in Heaven, with God the Father.

> So then the Lord **Jesus**, after he had spoken to them, **was taken *up* into heaven and sat down at the right hand of God.** (Mark 16:19 ESV)

> **[Jesus] has gone into heaven** and is at the right hand of God, with angels, authorities, and powers having been subjected to him. (1 Peter 3:22 ESV)

So the Bible actually seems to indicate that the righteous no longer inhabit an assigned region in Hades, but rather will travel to be with Jesus, up in God's heavenly kingdom. There will be many others there as well, just as Lazarus dined with Abraham in Jesus' parable, and it will be known as a paradise, a place of total bliss. and fellowship in the presence of God and all other inhabitants, similar to the experience of Eden so long ago. Notice also the direction of travel in Mark 16 - *upward*. While some might argue that the upward and downward trajectory described in the Bible can be attributed solely to the cosmological model in the mindset of the Biblical authors, that certainly doesn't preclude the possibility that there is an underlying truth about the relationship between these locations in the spiritual realm, nor does it prevent God from presenting these experiences in such a way that He chooses. So let's not get caught up in an overanalysis of the limited cosmological knowledge of the Biblical authors and instead simply let the text speak for itself.

So just as Sheol provides context for DNDEs, it seems to me that the Biblical description of Paradise, where Jesus currently resides at the right hand of the Father, fits perfectly with the realm of pleasant NDEs. A spiritual reality beyond our material universe, an upward trajectory of travel to meet with Jesus, a Being who radiates a brilliant light, complete peace, overwhelming self-sacrificial love, and perfect fellowship with friends, family, and loved ones in the same state of existence. This is the backdrop for the state of spiritual freedom - the realm of truly pleasant NDEs.

~ Putting it All Together ~

Therefore, the true Biblical teaching of the human condition immediately after death tells the story of a spiritual existence in a dichotomy between freedom in Paradise with Jesus or confinement in Sheol. This teaching is precisely what we have been able to infer directly from the NDE evidence. And since we have very strong reasons to believe that the Christian worldview is indeed true, it only further corroborates the framework revealed by the NDEs themselves.

So, given the context of Biblical teaching, combined with the evidence revealed by NDEs, we can update our framework accordingly.

Every NDE takes place either in Paradise or in Sheol. In Paradise, the human soul exists in the comforting presence of Jesus - radiating an immense light from His bodily form - overwhelmed by His love and compassion. Those who ascend to this state are free to fellowship and interact with others, being fully known and understood, without judgment, shame, or sorrow. In Sheol, the human soul exists in the agony of solitary confinement, isolated from the love and presence of God, but also isolated from those whom they loved in life. Those who descend to this state will reside in cubic cells along the outer perimeter of the pit and may be visited by malevolent spiritual beings - the assembly of Rephaim - and suffer under their insidious tortures. While those in Paradise are free to make continuous journeys back to their bodies before being resuscitated, those in Sheol may not have the same freedom, often simply waking up in their bodies without a return journey. The experience in Sheol may be one of isolation in a void or vast barren environment, it may consist of terrifying and painful encounters with the Rephaim, or it may be somewhere in between, possibly including some sort of deceptively pleasant interaction with these malevolent spiritual beings. The virtual nature of reality within the cubic cell can result in nonsensical and discontinuous changes of location or objects within the scene. Since the Rephaim can change form and appearance within the cell, it is possible for an NDEr in Sheol to be deceived into believing they are communicating with someone when in fact they are not. The messages and "truths" revealed by the Rephaim are not to be trusted and must be viewed with a healthy dose of skepticism.

Obviously, this expanded description of the framework is based on the truth of the Christian worldview. Although I believe I've made a reasonable case for that truth in this chapter, I realize that many will reject my conclusion and therefore may be unwilling to accept my interpretation of the evidence. Regardless of where you land on this spectrum, I hope that if you've made it this far into the book, you've come to see the framework of spiritual freedom and spiritual confinement as a comprehensive lens through which to view all NDEs. And I hope that if you choose to create your own explanation for that framework, you'll make an honest assessment of its explanatory power and scope compared to what I've described here.

7

WHY??

Although I never really got into the Harry Potter book series growing up, mainly because they were first released just as I was entering high school and starting to get busy with clubs and activities, I have seen some of the earlier movies. And now that my kids are getting older, I expect they'll be added to the pool of Friday Family Movies in the very near future. This time, however, will be different for me, because I know the story, I know the ending, and I know all the plot twists along the way. Granted, the movies are a little formulaic and predictable at times, but I do remember one plot twist in particular that caught me completely off guard. It comes from the Prisoner of Azkaban, which I originally saw only because I tend to enjoy the acting talents of Gary Oldman.

~ SPOILER ALERT ~

Keep in mind, I hadn't read the books, so all I knew about Sirius Black was that he was in prison for murdering a bunch of people, that he worked for Voldemort, and that he was the one who betrayed Harry's parents to the evil wizard, resulting in their deaths. Throughout the entire film, the actions of Sirius, the creepy dementors, and the giant black dog, all felt like threats to our protagonist group of teenage friends. I really wanted them to catch Sirius and bring him to justice for all the evil he had done.

But then, I found out that Sirius didn't actually kill all those people - he was innocent and wrongly imprisoned. He wasn't a spy for Voldemort, and he didn't betray Harry's parents. It was actually Peter Pettigrew who did all of those things, and he had been disguised as Ron Weasley's rat, Scabbers. In reality, Sirius Black recognized Scabbers as Pettigrew in a newspaper photograph, and knew the threat he posed to Harry, which gave him the will to escape from prison. All along, his motives were not to escape and finish the evil work he had started, but rather to avenge the evil work for which he had been framed, and to protect his godson, Harry Potter. It's amazing how understanding the reason and purpose behind one's actions can completely change our perspective on things. I find that if we don't fully understand that reason or purpose, it can often lead us to the wrong conclusions, as was the case with me and Sirius Black.

~ END OF SPOILERS ~

This chapter is entirely devoted to the question of *why*. Why does only a small percentage of the population have NDEs? Why does the Land Best Forgotten exist? Why does it contain individual cubic cells? Why do some experience demonic torture and others are just alone in a void? Why would a loving God ever send anyone to such a place? Understanding the *why* is important, because when we don't fully understand the reason or purpose for something, it can often lead us to the wrong conclusions.

I am going to be completely honest with you here. When I began to really study the concepts of the afterlife, when I began to research Heaven, Hell, and the new creation concepts established in the Bible, I went through several rounds of doubt, uncertainty, and confusion. I had to fight my own preconceived notions, and allow myself to simply sit back and let the Biblical text speak for itself. It's a difficult process, and I know you may experience a similar struggle as we work through this together. But I wanted to at least share with you the process of my own education here, and just lay out for you where I have landed on these big questions. I call these *responses*, rather than *answers*, because I don't feel that I have the authority to dogmatically assert my own thoughts here as the final answer to these questions. Nonetheless, this study has helped me to gain a better understanding of the Biblical concepts of spiritual reality, so I'd like to share with you what I've discovered along the way.

~ Why Hell ~

I put this one first because it's a big one, and to understand it you need a basic understanding of the overarching narrative of the Bible itself. This knowledge will be a prerequisite for understanding the responses to later questions. So let's just bite the bullet and tackle this one head on.

I feel that so many people, Christians included, misunderstand the purpose for Hell because of a fundamental misunderstanding or poor framing of the overarching Biblical narrative. For many, the Bible is seen as nothing more than a self-help book, a place to pick up a few helpful nuggets of information about how to live a good life, a place to find advice in times of uncertainty, a catalog of good examples for us to model and follow in our own lives. But then, when we read the stories of death and destruction, when we find instructions that don't match our own definitions of "good" and "loving," when flipping the Bible open to a random verse doesn't reveal any more wisdom than a magic 8-ball, we begin to wonder why we're referencing this book at all. It's clearly not serving its intended purpose.

Plus, there's this "god" in there who is trying to tell us how to live our lives and threatening to throw us into a burning pit of despair if we don't follow all of his buzz-kill rules. Is it really "good news" that this god has offered to save us from what he will do to us if we don't let him save us? We see this "turn or burn" philosophy as completely incompatible with the idea of a loving God. Therefore, our conclusion is either that He won't really send us to Hell, or that none of it exists at all, and the logical inconsistency is only due to the inability of the human mind to create a coherent story in its attempt to control the masses through the formation of a new religion.

But I've learned that this is not the purpose of the Bible at all. And when we don't fully understand the reason or purpose for something, it can often lead us to the wrong conclusions. So I'd like to offer you a new 10,000-foot view of the Biblical metanarrative.

The Bible begins with the account of a spiritual Being powerful enough to create order out of chaos, to create light out of darkness, to separate water from dry land, and to form plants and animals from the raw materials of the universe. And at the pinnacle of this Being's creative endeavors, It creates humanity, man and woman, to live alongside the plants and animals.

However, It sets humanity apart from the animals, bestowing upon us Its very own image, and assigning us our primary role in this new creation - to cultivate and subdue the Earth. We were created with the express purpose of tending and ruling our corner of creation on this Being's behalf, harnessing the natural resources built into our planet and using them for the benefit of all life on Earth. We are to take the beauty and order created by this Being and create from it even more order and beauty, to be this Being's representatives and rulers over Its beautiful created world.

And this Being, who goes by the name Yahweh, who claims to be the one and only eternal, uncreated, all-powerful "God" in existence, gave humanity the freedom to choose how we would rule. Would we follow God, modeling our thoughts, works, and behaviors after what He says is good, relying on Him to help us learn what is truly good and what is truly evil? Or would we usurp God's power and create our own definitions of good and evil, ruling on our own terms, and attempting to become gods in our own right. Unfortunately, humanity has consistently chosen the latter, and the results have been catastrophic.

Since that time, selfishness, reckless ambition, greed, lust, malice, slander, among many other vices, have become the foundations of human civilization; a far cry from the beauty of the paradise we once inhabited. Nation fights nation in a never-ending struggle for *more*: more land, more resources, more power!

At the height of human rebellion, when power-hungry men presumptuously attempted to elevate themselves to the heavens and establish their divine status, God brought division among them and scattered them throughout the world. And it was at this time that He gave up on the idea of bringing His kingdom to the entire world through a single, unified human race and instead delegated rule and authority over the now-divided human nations to lesser spiritual beings. But these beings, in their own lust for power and worship, also rebelled against God and decided to rule their kingdoms according to their own definitions of good and evil, just as mankind had done in the garden.

Then God chose one couple whom He would use to create an entirely new nation, a nation that would model what it looks like to live differently than these worldly kingdoms. A nation that would bring forth a new humanity capable of loving God, obeying His commandments, and serving all mankind with a selfless, sacrificial love under which creation could flourish once again. At that moment, God began the process of building *His* kingdom in the midst of the broken and shattered human condition, and He used this one nation to show the world what that could look like.

Unfortunately, this nation could not live up to the standard; it consistently failed to represent God among the other nations. Its leaders and rulers sought after power and greed, and the people lived under the same injustices as every other kingdom in the world. This kingdom was God's kingdom in name only, but nowhere near what His true kingdom could be. It became clear that only a change in the hearts of men would allow the people to truly love God and live according to the laws of His kingdom.

So God raised up a small group of prophets through whom He delivered warnings of impending judgment and destruction. If this nation, living under the constant guidance and instruction of God Himself, could not live up to the standard of His kingdom and show the world what it looks like to live according to His definitions of good and evil, if they were indistinguishable from the other kingdoms of this world, then there is no reason to sustain them as a city on a hill. A lighthouse can only serve its intended purpose when the light shines bright, and this nation was dark indeed.

God allowed powerful enemies to descend upon this nation, conquer its capital cities, and carry its people off into exile as captives of the worldly kingdoms which they so stubbornly chose to imitate. But even in the darkness of exile, in the chaos of captivity, God brought a word of hope to this nation.

Their prophets foretold of a future leader of their people, one who would persevere where they had failed, who would change the hearts of the people so that they would finally choose

135

to love God and to love one another. This leader would usher in God's true kingdom here on Earth, restoring creation to its rightful owner and allowing it to flourish once again, with God and man ruling together, as it was meant to be in the beginning.

But then the Old Testament ended, the prophets died, and nothing happened for hundreds of years until we're introduced to a man who was born into this nation: Jesus of Nazareth. He not only lived up to the standards of God's kingdom, He claimed to be the one ushering it into existence. He turned the social order of this world on its head by teaching others that the kingdom of God would gain power and momentum through service and sacrifice rather than through the evils of worldly strength and domination. And He lived out this principle to the point of His own execution, where His sacrifice and love for humanity finally overcame the evil that plagues our world, and now offers us a road to freedom from our exile in the kingdoms of this world.

When mankind was driven out of God's kingdom in Genesis chapter 3, God placed cherubim and a flaming sword to block the entrance to the garden paradise. This was to indicate that anyone who tried to re-enter God's kingdom would die before they even got in the front door. Therefore, we needed someone else to pay our entrance fee if we ever hoped to rejoin God's kingdom. And that was precisely the purpose of Jesus' death on the cross. He paid our entrance fee, He absolved us of debt incurred when we decided to live life by our own rules, He embraced death in our place, just as He said He would. And so that we could have confidence in the truth of Jesus' claims, God vindicated Jesus by publicly raising Him from the dead, making

Him not only the Lord and ruler of the coming kingdom, but also the first human resurrected into its membership. Now all of humanity has the opportunity to leave behind our exilic captivity in the kingdoms of this world and become citizens of God's kingdom once again. As we do so, God's Spirit will dwell within us, changing our hearts, giving us the power to choose selflessness and sacrificial love, and allowing us to live as we were meant to live in the first place.

The rest of the New Testament consists of letters among the early followers of Jesus, instructing each other to remain steadfast and faithful to the kingdom of God, even in the face of persecution and death. The Greek word they use for "gospel" is *euangelion*, which is a proclamation of good news. But it's not just generic good news, like saving a kitten from a tree. In using this word, the apostles are pointing back to the Septuagint translation of Isaiah 52:7, where the verb *euangelizo* describes a courrier running to bring the good news to Zion that, "Our God Reigns!" It is a call to the people to come and celebrate, the king has returned victorious. So the gospel of Jesus, in its full context, is more than Jesus "dying for our sins," more than being "saved from Hell," more than "going to Heaven when we die." It is a proclamation that Jesus has prevailed over death, that the kingdom of God is finally here, and that all of us can now freely escape from our corrupt worldly kingdoms and join the kingdom of God thanks to the atoning sacrifice of Jesus.

The last book of the Bible speaks of the revelation of this King Jesus. It says that at some point in the future He will establish God's complete kingdom here on Earth, restoring all of creation to its rightful owner and allowing it to flourish once again, with God and man ruling together as it was meant to be since the beginning. And just as the nation of Israel waited patiently for their promised future leader, so Christians now wait patiently for the day when Jesus is revealed as the one true God and ruler over all creation, when His kingdom comes here on Earth as it is in Heaven.

The hope of the Christian worldview is not a disembodied spiritual state as experienced in NDEs, but rather a resurrection into material bodies and a restoration into a renewed and perfected creation; a world like this one, with skiing and surfing, with picnics and dinner parties, with friends, family, and loved ones. Together in perfect community, living out the principles of service and sacrificial love for the good of all who live here. Therefore, our ultimate destiny is not Heaven, but Paradise; a worldwide Garden of Eden where God and mankind live together in perfect harmony. It is that utopian world that we all long for and continually fail to create for ourselves. Christians look forward to the day when God will change the hearts of all who live in His kingdom so that we can finally realize this perfect society free of tears, sorrow, and pain.

At that time in the future, Jesus will finally eliminate all sin and death, end all suffering, and banish all evil to a place the Bible calls "the lake of fire," also called Hell, though different from the present Sheol, which is the Land Best Forgotten. Therefore, according to the Bible, Hell is nothing more than a prison. It is a place where all evil is confined so that it can no longer corrupt the newly restored creation. In God's kingdom, there will be no more pain, no more sorrow, no more tears, so anyone who has the potential to hurt others must remain in exile outside the kingdom. The place of this exile is Hell. It is the only viable means of protecting the new creation from the continuing evils that will always emanate from the hearts of a rebellious human nature.

Consider our own society. We uphold certain laws that our citizens must obey in order to maintain a thriving and prosperous society where our citizens feel safe and cared for. And when someone deliberately and maliciously breaks those laws, we send him to jail. We lock him up in a prison to protect the citizens outside the walls, and we confine him to his individual cell to protect the other inmates in the prison with him. Since this person is incapable of living according to the law of the land, he must remain in prison until he dies or is no longer a threat to society. This is the exact image and purpose of Hell.

A restored creation without Hell is like a society without prisons. Those who choose to violate the laws of the land would wreak havoc on the innocent members of society. This is unsafe for the citizens, unfair to those who obey the law, and it makes the leaders of that society either evil or incompetent for allowing such atrocities to continue unchecked. If this were allowed to happen in the restored creation, then that future utopia would be no better off than we are today.

Therefore, it seems to me that Hell must exist, and God must fill it with all beings capable of harming others, so that the union of God's heavenly kingdom and our restored material universe can be free of all tears, sorrow, and pain. Our biggest problem is that as exiles in kingdoms of this world, living by our own rules, choosing our own definitions of good and evil, we all have the capacity to harm others, and left to our own devices, we have no hope of changing our rebellious behavior. So we are all bound for the prison called Hell when our life here is complete.

And that is precisely why God sends His Spirit to live within His kingdom followers, to change them and empower them to choose the ways of selflessness and sacrificial love. God didn't leave us to suffer our prison sentence, but rather established a rehabilitation program through which He can change our hearts and minds. In doing so, He not only uses us to change our present world for the better, but also prepares us to live in that future Utopia, saving us not only from ourselves and each other, but also from our future destiny in that prison called Hell.

~ WHY FIRE ~

But if Hell is just a prison, why does the Bible so often use the language of fire to describe it? Am I just trying to water down the idea of Hell to make it more palatable than the blazing inferno that it really is? Here is what I discovered.

When we read the word "fire" in the New Testament, it's a translation of the Greek word *pyr*, which occurs a total of 74 times in the New Testament. However, only 29 of these instances are part of explicit references to the concept of Hell. Furthermore, 14 of those 29 occur in parallel accounts of the same teachings in the four different gospels. So while fire is certainly an important image when it comes to Hell, it's actually not as common as many believe.

In addition, if we look at the remaining verses relevant to fire and Hell, the vast majority of them are used to describe the destruction of things that are not good for serving their intended purpose. For example, in Matthew 3:10, 7:19, and Luke 3:9, Hell is said to be analogous to cutting down trees that do not bear fruit and burning them because they can no longer serve their intended purpose. In Matthew 3:12, Hell is compared to taking the wheat grains from the harvest and then throwing the husks and chaff into the fire because they have no nutritional value. In Matthew 13:40,42, Mark 9:43-49, and Luke 3:17, Hell is compared to separating the grain from the weeds and then throwing the weeds into the fire because they cannot be used for food. In Matthew 13:50, Hell is compared to sorting fish and throwing out those that are not good for eating.

In these examples, the fire is not a means of tormenting the trees or plants, but is simply a means of eliminating things that can no longer be of use, while the parts that are retained continue to provide food and life for others. Therefore, the Bible does not necessarily indicate that Hell is an endless inferno of blazing torment for those trapped in it, but rather uses the imagery of fire as a means of getting rid of things that can no longer benefit the flourishing of life. If our purpose is to love God and to truly love others sacrificially as God would, then anyone who would bring harm or suffering to others is not fit to fulfill that purpose. It is for this reason that we are destined for the "fire" of Hell like the chaff, weeds, and rotten fish.

Although Revelation 14:10 refers to the followers of the Antichrist (a.k.a. the beast) being tormented with fire and brimstone, there are no other specific passages concerning hellfire that indicate that the inhabitants of Hell will exist in a literal flame. Rather, the fire serves as a metaphor to describe the fate of all beings who are incapable of living in such a way that they will never cause harm or pain to others. Since there are numerous Biblical references to Sheol or Hades that do not mention fire at all (Genesis 37:35, Numbers 16:30, 2 Samuel 22:6, 1 Kings 2:6, Job 17:16, Psalms 139:8, Isaiah 14:11,15, Jonah 2:2, Matthew 11:23, Luke 10:15, 1 Corinthians 15:55, Revelation 1:18, and many more), we must come to terms with the idea that the actual ontology of Hell may be much more complex than the oversimplified caricature of blazing hellfire.

~ WHY WEEPING AND GNASHING ~

Even if Hell is not a blazing inferno, why did Jesus say that its inhabitants will weep and gnash their teeth? Doesn't this indicate that these people will be in intense physical pain, as one would expect from a never-ending fire? That's how I used to look at this phrase. But after a more careful word study, I've come to a different conclusion.

In all of these phrases, the Greek word for gnashing is *brygmos*. This word occurs only seven times in the entire New Testament, all of them within the context of this particular phrase spoken by Jesus. So at first it was a little difficult for me to get a proper idea of what it was trying to convey. However, in the Septuagint, this word appears in Proverbs 19:12, which tells us that the wrath of the king is like the growling [*brygmos*] of a lion. So the Greek-speaking Jews who wrote the Septuagint associated this word with the wrath of a king and the growl of a lion. When we picture these two images in our minds, what emotion do you think accompanies them? For me, the overarching theme is anger.

The fury of a king bubbling up into an outburst of wrath, like the angry growl of an irritated lion.

Satisfied with this understanding, I moved on to "weeping," which is expressed by the Greek word *klauthmos*. Outside of these phrases, where it is paired with gnashing of teeth, this word appears in only two other places. In Matthew 2:18, when King Herod executes all Israelite male children under the age of two, the author refers to a prophecy in Jeremiah 31:15 that speaks of a heartbroken woman weeping [*klauthmos*] and lamenting the death of her children. Likewise, in Acts 20:37, when the church leaders from Ephesus came to visit Paul in Miletus, there was much weeping [*klauthmos*] as they bid him farewell and accompanied him to his ship bound for Jerusalem. In both cases, this word is applied to those who are experiencing deep sadness at the loss of those they love. This seems to me to represent the emotion of sorrow. The sorrow of losing a child; the sorrow of saying goodbye to a dear friend, perhaps for the last time.

So when I look at these words together in the same sentence, it seems to me that the best description of the underlying emotion is grief. I don't think Jesus is referring to physical pain at all, but rather an emotional torment that sends us into the various stages of grief. I have come to believe that Jesus is describing for us the mental and emotional state of what it will be like to arrive in that prison called Hell, isolated from our loved ones, left to ruminate on the actions that brought us to this desolate existence, and feeding our anger and hatred of the system that resulted in our hopeless sentence. We will experience sorrow; we will experience anger; there will be weeping and gnashing of teeth.

~ Why Not Just Forgive ~

So if Jesus died for the sins of the world, if he paid our ticket to get back into the kingdom, why wouldn't God just forgive all the sins of all people and bring everyone into His kingdom? This question in particular is why I started using the kingdom framework to describe our condition and the metanarrative of the Bible. Because I used to think in terms of "going to Heaven" when we die, and I wondered why God didn't just proactively apply that forgiveness to all people, thereby allowing all people to "go to Heaven." But when I learned to rephrase the question in terms of kingdoms, the response became much clearer to me.

I have come to see Jesus' sacrifice as sufficient to cover the sins of the whole world, but all this means is that Jesus is now standing at the front gate of God's kingdom with tickets in hand, a gate that only He could open, having done so through His sacrificial death on the cross. It is still up to us to approach the gate, humbly accept the ticket, and then choose to enter God's kingdom by living a life of repentance and following Jesus' example of service and sacrificial love for others.

There are some who don't want to have anything to do with Jesus or God's kingdom, so they are content to stay in their own kingdom, far from the gate where Jesus resides. There are some who are attracted by the benefits of living in the kingdom, but they decide that it is not for them, and they find themselves drawn back into the kingdoms of the world. But only those who choose to enter the kingdom of God in this life through the free gift offered by Jesus, regardless of our own good deeds or works in life, will be on the path to rehabilitation and therefore be able to live in the restored creation with a renewed nature.

So the issue is not a lack of forgiveness on the part of God, but rather a lack of desire or initiative on the part of the individual. It's a 2-way street, and it's up to us to reach out and accept the gift. Forgiveness is on the table, but it comes with entry into His kingdom, not just as a blanket to be applied to all of creation. And since God has given us the freedom to choose how we live our lives, He will honor our choice to enter His kingdom or to remain as we are. He will not force anyone to enter *His* kingdom and live under *His* rules for a prosperous and peaceful society.

But we tend to like our lives. It works for us. Things are going well. We don't want to give up certain behaviors or habits. We want to be seen as cool or edgy. We want to be the master of our own destiny, the ruler of our own world, without some overbearing "god" telling us what to do or how to live.

And so God will give us exactly what we want. He will give us our own individual cell in a prison called Hell, our own little world where we can rule as a god. A place without God's overbearing presence or rules. But as anyone who has been sentenced to solitary confinement will tell you, being completely alone with nothing but your own thoughts, your own grief and regret, your own pain over losing connection with those you love, is a greater torment than any hellfire could ever inflict.

I hope the above responses have been helpful to you in gaining a better understanding of why Hell exists and why it is described as it is in the Bible. I feel that the lens of kingdoms can give us a much better understanding of our current state and the stakes on the table before us; it has certainly been a helpful framework for me, and I hope you have found value in exploring it. But now let's switch gears and talk a little more about NDEs and the Land Best Forgotten.

~ WHY NDEs ~

I guess the cat is out of the bag. I am a Christian. And yes, I was a Christian before my research into NDEs. Although I was raised in a Christian household, as was pretty typical for many suburban Midwesterners in the 90's, I underwent what I would also call a "typical" transition to apatheism in my mid 20's. I may have held on to the traditional morals of my upbringing, and I may have identified as "Christian," but I certainly had not fully embraced it, had not devoted time to studying its truth claims, and had no idea that there was such a vast field of study devoted to the historicity and logical cogency of the worldview.

It was this evidence and these arguments that convinced me that Christianity was true, that I could become a person who lived less selfishly and more sacrificially by allowing God to transform me, that the Creator of the universe cared enough about me to put on the frailty of the human condition, to live a life full of pain and hardship, and to suffer one of the most agonizing executions in human history. And now my hope is that one day God will raise me and all my friends and family who are also part of His kingdom to be part of a new creation, a restored creation with all the beauty of our present world but without all the pain and suffering. And between my earthly death and that future day when God finally restores our universe to a state of paradise, I look forward to being "present with the Lord," to abiding in the love and fellowship of God and all other beings in His kingdom.

This intermediate state of disembodied existence in God's heavenly kingdom, in the presence of the Creator of the universe, energized by God's abundance of unconditional love, present with friends and family as we rest in the comfort and protection of a perfectly loving Father, is precisely the state experienced by those who have a near-death experience. At least, that's how I've come to see it. I believe that the state of spiritual freedom is only a taste of the love and beauty we can expect to find in the presence of God. I do not believe it is our *final* destination, which is instead a resurrected existence in a new creation where God's presence is just as palpable. But I *do* believe it is a preview of a life lived in the intimate presence of God.

Likewise, I believe that the disembodied existence in an isolated prison cell, separated from God, removed from His loving presence, isolated from friends and family, in a state of grief, tormented by regret and the pain we carry within us, is precisely the state experienced by those who have a distressing near-death experience. I believe that the state of spiritual confinement is only a taste of the loneliness and despair we can expect to find in a place completely devoid of the loving presence of God. It is a preview of a life lived utterly alone, trapped with only the pain and anger we carry within, without connection, without relationship, without hope.

After years of studying the truth claims and teachings of the Bible, and years of reading and reflecting on NDEs, I have come to believe that God allows people to experience NDEs precisely to give us confidence in life after death and to give us the opportunity to respond to that evidence. As He does with so many other things, He has given us just enough evidence to justify the faith and belief of those who truly love Him and want to be a part of His kingdom, but has left just enough ambiguity to allow those who do not want to be a part of His kingdom to feel satisfied in their rejection.

Think about how you felt in the early chapters of this book, reading first-hand accounts of the beauty of pleasant NDEs and the pain and agony of DNDEs. Even without the baggage of associating them with a particular worldview, NDEs give us a very good reason to believe in life after death, to believe that the afterlife could be one of unfathomable peace and love, or one of excruciating emotional pain and anguish. The value of this evidence cannot be overstated. If we follow this evidence objectively, it should at least cause us to question any kind of worldview that denies the existence of an immaterial or spiritual reality. And if it doesn't, then perhaps this reveals to us our true motivation to be masters of our own destiny, on our own terms, with our own definition of good and evil. In that case, we shouldn't be surprised to find ourselves locked in a cell in Sheol.

Hebrews 11:1 says, "Faith is the assurance of things hoped for, the conviction of things not seen. (ESV)" It is not blind, it does not require us to check our intellect at the door. Rather, it is informed by the evidence all around us. In my opinion, NDEs serve this very purpose. They offer conviction of an existence we cannot see, a spiritual reality that overlaps with our material existence, filled with other spiritual beings, both loving and malevolent, and an all-knowing, all-loving, personal God who loves us and wants to share His kingdom with us. NDEs offer the assurance of a spiritual rest for those in God's kingdom, a time when we will be "absent the body and present with the Lord," and they give us all the more reason to believe that, like Jesus, we will be raised from the dead, given new physical bodies, and exist forever in God's kingdom when it is reunited with our physical creation, on Earth as it is in Heaven.

So I've come to believe that NDEs are simply a gift from God, a preview of what is to come after death, the good, the bad, and everything in between, so that we can be confident in our decision to forsake the kingdoms of this world in favor of the kingdom of God.

~ WHY ARE NDEs RARE ~

Those who reject the spiritual or transcendental nature of NDEs in favor of a more materialistic explanation often point to the fact that most people who die don't have NDEs. If I understand their argument correctly, the fact that some people simply lose time between death and resuscitation is best explained by some physical predisposition, psychological state, or deeply held belief on the part of those who do have an NDE. In this way, the NDE is just something made up in the mind of the individual, and those who don't have an NDE simply don't hold such beliefs or live in such a state. But the proponents of this theory have no proposed mechanism to divide the population along these lines of NDErs and non-NDErs. And such a theory would still fall woefully short of explaining the myriad of events observed through the veridical perception of NDErs, as highlighted earlier in this book.

However, when we look through the lens of the Christian worldview, it seems to me that the rarity of NDEs actually makes a lot of sense. Throughout the entire Biblical story, there are only a few times when God Himself steps in to take significant action. If you really read the text, when God makes big moves in orchestrating events in the world, He does so primarily through human actors. Like the ten plagues of Egypt - certainly orchestrated by God, but actually delivered and executed by Moses. Or the judgment on Israel and the destruction of Jerusalem - carried out by Babylon. And the prophetic calls to repentance or messages of hope found in Isaiah and other prophets - all spoken to the people through fellow human beings. Nowhere in the Bible does God just sit on a high mountain and drop some big data dump on anyone who happens to be passing by. He works through human experience, and through a small number of people at that.

I have come to believe that NDEs work in essentially the same way. If God wants to use NDEs for our benefit, as a source of information about the existence and nature of an afterlife, then it would make perfect sense that He would choose only a small number of people through whom to deliver this message. In essence, NDErs have been offered the opportunity to serve as prophets, revealing to others an aspect of God's creation that most of us won't see until our lives are over. Just like Moses, Elijah, Jeremiah, Jonah, Isaiah and many others, these people have been chosen by God to receive a revelation of information from Him and now have the opportunity to play a role in helping others find their way back to God's kingdom. Since God consistently chooses only a small number of people to serve as this prophetic voice in the world, it makes perfect sense that NDEs would be rare.

Furthermore, I believe that the rarity of NDEs actually demonstrates a degree of sovereignty over life and death that would be cheapened if everyone had an NDE at the time of their death. If everyone had an NDE when they died, it would make the afterlife look completely uncontrolled and natural, like a ball rolling down a hill. The laws of nature simply dictate what happens next, with no need for intervention or supervision. However, by choosing to give some people an NDE and allowing others to simply experience a loss of time, God is demonstrating that He is in control, that He can and will choose what happens to you at the time of your death, and that He has complete power over the entirety of your life, this one and the next. In my opinion, this not only demonstrates God's sovereignty, but it should also motivate us to choose whether or not we really want to be in God's kingdom, knowing full well how that decision will affect our next life.

Finally, I believe NDEs are rare because God knows who will or will not be impacted for His kingdom through the experience. For example, God knew that Bryan would come back from his experience and go on to write a very powerful book, serve in a prison ministry, and work to reach many in his community for His kingdom. This single NDE has had a tremendous ripple effect, helping others find the conviction they need to remain convinced of their faith. I believe some people are given an NDE as part of their own path to joining God's kingdom, and I believe others are given an NDE simply so they can tell others about it and thus bring more people into His kingdom. However, I believe God knows who would not, or need not, be convinced by the experience, who would not tell others about the experience, and even those who might use it as a weapon to harm others. In these cases, and I'm sure for many other reasons, it seems to me that God is simply depriving such people of a transcendental experience, giving them only the feeling of time lost.

So in the end, the rarity of NDEs doesn't really seem unexpected in light of the Christian worldview. In fact, it's perfectly consistent with the nature of God and His patterns of behavior as described in the Bible. The way I see it, getting a glimpse of the afterlife is an amazing blessing for us, and I'm just glad that God gave it to *any* of us at all, when He certainly didn't have to. To me, the rarity of NDEs is yet another in a myriad of examples where God provides just enough evidence to allow those who want to be a part of His kingdom to feel justified in their conclusions, but leaves just enough ambiguity to allow those who do not want to join His kingdom to feel justified as well.

~ WHY CUBES ~

After my years of NDE study and continued reflection on this framework, I truly believe that the prison analogy is one of the best ways to understand Hell and how it plays into the metanarrative of the Bible. Although the Bible doesn't explicitly say that individuals will be placed in their own cells within this prison, I believe, based on the information revealed to Bryan in his NDE, that Hell does indeed contain cells, and I believe that this reality fits perfectly with the Biblical concept of proportional justice, meaning God's judgment will be proportional to our offenses in life.

> And that servant who knew his master's will but did not get ready or act according to his will, will receive a **severe beating**. But the one who did not know, and did what deserved a beating, will receive a **light beating**. Everyone to whom much was given, of him much will be required, and from him to whom they entrusted much, they will demand the more. (Luke 12:47-48 ESV)

> Truly, I say to you, it will be **more bearable** on the day of judgment for the land of Sodom and Gomorrah than for that town. (Matthew 10:15 ESV)

Notice that in both of these teachings, Jesus describes different degrees of punishment because the two groups handled what was entrusted to them differently. But when it comes to Hell, how would differing degrees of punishment actually be accomplished if not through the use of individual cells? Let's think through some alternative possibilities and follow them to their logical conclusion to see if they fit with the concept of proportional justice.

First, let's consider the model of Dante's Inferno. If all people were simply confined to a fiery pit, doomed to burn to ashes for all eternity, how could that be proportional? Jesus said that the cities that wouldn't receive His apostles or listen to their words would be worse off than those who lived in Sodom and Gomorrah. But how can that be if they're all just sitting in a giant furnace forever? If this model is true, then the fate of Hitler is no different from that of Gandhi. Does that seem proportional? I don't think so.

Or what if there weren't really any fires, but instead all the inhabitants lived together in one big, massive pit or cave, as is often the case in cartoon depictions of Hell. In this model, wouldn't the more evil and devious inhabitants be free to set up gangs and power structures that could take advantage of the more meek and timid inhabitants? Wouldn't it be the most evil person or demon who would rise to the top of this devious organizational structure and essentially rule with an iron fist over everyone else in that realm? In a truly proportional system, shouldn't it be the more evil people who receive more severe punishments rather than living the good life at the top of the food chain? I just can't reconcile this notion of Hell with the concept of proportional justice.

But individual cells...that's another story entirely. With each person confined to their own cell, they are not only protected from mistreatment by those who are more devious or powerful, but they are also prevented from mistreating those who are less devious or powerful than they are. This immediately removes the potential for power structures, for organized hierarchies, that could take advantage of others and perpetuate the evils of oppression into eternity. But since all people receive the same fate, namely confinement in their own cell, is it really proportional? I believe it is indeed.

There is a moment in Season 1, Episode 4 of the Netflix show Lost in Space when Don West bursts the bubble of utopian fantasies about Alpha Centauri, because the problem with society lies within the people themselves. "Whatever people think they're running from on Earth, they're just bringing it all with them," he exclaims with insightful cynicism. And that idea is precisely why I think the cells in Hell can be considered proportional.

Whatever evil people have done in their lives, whatever hatred and anger they have cultivated in their hearts, whatever betrayal they have committed, whatever pain they have caused, that stays with them in the cell. These actions and the regrets associated with them create a storm of emotional distress, sorrow, and torment within them. In this way, inside the small world of your own cell, you literally reap what you sow. Those who sow more evil bring it all into their cell, ammunition for the onslaught of emotional torment that inevitably follows. And those who cultivate a more loving and gracious life would carry a lighter burden, perhaps only regretting the decision not to join God's kingdom and avoid such desolate isolation.

Or we could rephrase this idea in terms of our kingdom analogy. As I've said before, part of the Biblical metanarrative tells of our exile in the kingdoms of the world, trying to carve out our own authority and dominion on our own terms, with our own definitions of good and evil. But when God's heavenly kingdom merges with our material universe to form a restored, new creation, there will be no place where we can be free to live that way. Everything on Earth, as it is in Heaven, will be under God's kingdom, living according to God's definitions of good and evil. But the cell provides a means of isolation from God's kingdom so that we can maintain our own rules and dominion. Our own little kingdom, population 1.

For my fellow tech geeks out there, think of it as a virtual machine on a computer. Have you ever installed a Windows or MacOS virtual machine on a Linux PC? Or vice-versa? Regardless of the operating system that occupies the entire hard drive, we can allocate a small portion of our disk space to an installation of a completely different operating system, with different rules for execution and a completely different user interface. Within its own isolated space, the virtual operating system is completely unaware of and protected from any rules that the parent operating system might impose everywhere else. In fact, it doesn't even know that such a parent operating system, with its entirely different set of rules and standards, exists beyond itself. However, the parent operating system remains aware of the virtual machine and supports it with its own physical resources.

So the cell offers not only protection from other inmates of Hell, but also protection from the overwhelming love and presence of God, from the constant reminder of His rules that we have come to despise, His definitions of good and evil. It offers each of its inhabitants their own little virtual machine, their own little space where they can live by their own rules and standards, where they can be masters of their own domain. But we also carry our own anger, our own hatred and pain, our own sorrow, forever tormented by the emotional baggage we have cultivated throughout our lives. And since all of us, living by our own flawed standards and behaviors, would remain capable of inflicting further pain and suffering on others, our virtual machine must be one of isolation, protecting us from each other and denying us the opportunity to hurt anyone else. Therefore, if our prison sentence in Hell is to be truly proportional to our deeds in life, it must exist within the confines of an individual cell, just as Bryan's NDE revealed.

~ Why Demonic Torture ~

I've saved this question for near the end, not only because it involves a lot of philosophical conjecture, but also because it ties together much of what we've discussed so far. I want to reiterate up front that it's entirely possible that my perspective and my responses here are wrong or misguided. But as of the writing of this section, it's been a few years since I developed this NDE framework, so I've had some time to reflect on the stories, read new ones, and learn more about the intermediate state after our death. So here I hope to just lay out my thoughts and feelings and explain how I came to my current conclusion.

To be abundantly clear, the full question at hand is: If the Land Best Forgotten is supposed to be a prison, with each individual isolated in his or her own cell, then why do some of the people who reside there experience horrific torture at the hands of foul, devious creatures? How could spiritual confinement bring only the emotional torment of loneliness to some, while it brings horrific forms of the most painful torture imaginable to others? This is a question I've spent a lot of time meditating and praying about as I've struggled to accept the reality of spiritual confinement as presented by the evidence of a vast number of distressing NDEs. And this is where I've ended up.

First, let me give you my thoughts on how the cells actually work. When I first read Bryan's book, I believed that it was these demonic creatures that controlled the virtual world inside the cells, as if they had an infinite number of funhouse environments that they could queue up on demand to invoke the worst kind of torture imaginable. But after much study and meditation, I have changed my mind.

I believe that the realities experienced within the cell are actually created by the human heart and mind, at least initially. As I've mentioned before, I believe that the cell offers its inhabitants a world in which they can live a life free from the influence of God, where they can create their own rules and live according to their own definitions of good and evil. Remember the virtual machine analogy above? I believe that these cells are designed to take the thoughts, memories, and emotions of the individual and manifest them in some representative way. In essence, I believe that God has given us what we want - a world in which we can be god, a world that responds to our mental and emotional states. To me, this seems perfectly consistent with the idea of reaping what you sow, because the evil that you carry with you into the cell will manifest visibly, reminding you of the hurt and pain that you have caused others during your life.

In fact, I think we can see examples of this in Bryan's book. One such example would have been the man who in life framed an innocent business rival for a crime for which he spent the rest of his life rotting in a prison cell. And for that man, his cell in the Land Best Forgotten looked just like the prison cell where his rival rotted in life. It seems to me that the world inside his cell manifested the evil actions of that man before his very eyes, forcing him to confront his own hurtful and evil actions, and reiterating the need for him to be locked in his own cell so that he could no longer hurt others as he had already done.

This would also explain why so many people in Bryan's book appear in settings that are familiar to them from life. For example, the woman from 19th century France and the ancient Aztec priest both lived in an environment that looked and felt somewhat like the time and place in which they lived their lives. I believe that this correlation between the world within the cell and the reality in which the person lived their life only further solidifies the idea that the cells reflect the individual within and are not directly controlled by the demons.

So, in my opinion, the cells are not really meant to be torture chambers, but simply reflect the heart and mind of the person inside. Whatever evil, hatred, malice, pain, regret, or other emotional baggage we may bring with us is manifested in the isolated world of the cell, reminding us of our own tendency toward painful actions. It's like Don West said, it's only as bad as the stuff we bring with us. And it is this emotional baggage that creates the inner emotional torment of hell, the torment that leads to weeping and gnashing of teeth.

But internal emotional *torment* is entirely different from external physical *torture*. So how does the latter come into play?

As I mentioned earlier, I have come to believe that the spiritual beings encountered in the Land Best Forgotten are very closely related to the Biblical Rephaim, those descendants of the Nephilim, the offspring of the unsanctioned relationships between the rebellious "sons of God" and human women. (If you're struggling with this idea, I highly recommend reading Michael Heiser's *The Unseen Realm*). They are the assembly that comes to greet the kings of Babylon and Assyria in the prophecies of Isaiah and Ezekiel. They are the dead souls of unrighteous, evil men who were corrupted by the lineage of rebellious spiritual beings. Because they were part-human and members of ungodly kingdoms, their destination after death must have been Sheol. However, because they were descended from the sons of God, and not directly from God through Adam, they have an almost demigod quality to them, and are therefore not confined in the same way as "purebred" humans. I believe this explains their freedom to roam around Sheol, entering and exiting the cubic cells at their disposal. This gives them the opportunity to do whatever horrible things they so desire to the humans held captive in the cells.

Furthermore, in our review of NDEs, it became clear that communication in this spiritual realm often occurs telepathically, without the need for spoken words, even in the domain of distressing NDEs. Remember, for example, the DNDE cited earlier in which the NDEr reported hearing his thoughts out loud, or the one in which the word "void" kept appearing in his mind. I believe these examples highlight for us the fact that these spiritual beings in Sheol can communicate with the captive humans through the same telepathic link described in so many other NDEs, which could explain how the beings might influence the environment or scene depicted in the cell. Here is how I have come to see this working.

The "void" is merely the empty construct for the world inside the cubic cell. It is a world that consists of nothing but your own mind. You are aware of your existence, present with your thoughts, but you have nothing or no one to interact with. As your mind begins to wander, the world inside your cube begins to manifest visible representations of your own thoughts and emotions. So, if you long to return home, you may begin to see landscapes or places that look exactly like home. But after a while, loneliness begins to set in, and you begin to fear that you are trapped in this place, somehow unable to escape this new reality. These distressing feelings then begin to alter the atmosphere inside your cube.

For example, recall again the case of the man whose environment looked like the prison cell where his corporate rival spent the rest of his life. I believe this man probably began his experience in a more neutral environment, but as he began to question why he was so alone and what he had done wrong to deserve such a bleak existence, thoughts of his actions and the guilt he felt about them crept into his mind and the scene changed. It began to reflect something he thought he deserved for his wicked actions in life. You reap what you sow.

But now let's bring the other spiritual beings into the picture. When they enter the cube, they become a part of your world. And through that telepathic connection, they may be able to influence your thoughts. Just as the word "void" kept popping into the mind of one of those DNDErs, what if they could plant other thoughts in your mind? What if they made you think of pink elephants? What if they made you remember some terrible thing you did in your life? I believe they can use this telepathic connection to influence your thoughts and feelings and thereby change the environment around you.

So if they bring to your mind a scene of hellfire, or introduce the idea of groups of people being torn to pieces, and those ideas take hold in your mind, then the cube will manifest that reality for you. Think of it like the movie Inception. They place ideas in your mind that evoke real emotional responses within you, and those feelings and ideas become a reality within the cell, indistinguishable from your own thoughts and feelings.

Perhaps they even change their appearance in this way; they simply put the idea of how they want to appear into your mind and the cubic cell makes it a reality. Or perhaps the cubic cell is also responding to their thoughts and feelings, overriding your virtual experience to cultivate an atmosphere of whatever devious form of terror and torture they can devise.

The point I want to make here is that I do not believe the cubic cells themselves were designed to be torture chambers. I believe they were designed to be a source of isolation for the protection of the inhabitant and other human inhabitants of Sheol. I believe they were designed to essentially allow the humans inside to create their own world according to their own definitions of good and evil, essentially giving them what they have always wanted - to be their own god, to rule their own kingdom.

But I also believe that the cells reflect and manifest a reality according to the heart and mind of the inhabitant, so that any evil they bring with them, any regret they carry, any grief that results from their bleak existence, is played out in their own personal world, tormenting them as long as they reside there. The torture described in many DNDEs only comes into play because of the other evil spiritual beings who reside in Sheol and who happen to have more power and freedom in that realm. They too are prisoners of Sheol, and out of their own malice and boredom, they pass the time by infiltrating the cells, thereby influencing the worlds within them, and inflicting all manner of terror and torture upon the helpless human souls residing in their solitary confinement.

In a way, this actually alleviates my own concerns about the Lake of Fire, the final destination for all who oppose the kingdom of God and would continue to spread pain and suffering within it. Just as individual cells in Sheol simultaneously remove the potential for power grabs by evil people and provide a means of proportional justice for all those confined within, I have come to believe that all spiritual beings, human or otherwise, will be confined to their own individual cells in the Lake of Fire. This means that the torture we observe in the DNDEs will not exist in the Lake of Fire. It seems to me that the Rephaim, or whatever we want to call these devious spiritual beings, confined to their own cells, will no longer be able to torture helpless human victims, but will instead be tormented by their own evil actions and all the pain they have caused, both in life and during their time in Sheol.

~ Why The Deception ~

If my framework is correct, if all NDEs take place either in Paradise with Jesus and the other righteous dead, or in Sheol, confined within a cubic cell that manifests for the NDEr his or her own personal experience, then there must be a large number of NDEs that are heavily based on deception. Looking back at some of the "in between" NDE stories, I have suggested that many of them actually occurred within a cell in Sheol, and that the reality presented was merely a manifestation of the cell itself. Like the woman who was trapped in a palace garden and told to wait until the day of final judgment. Or the man who met his father and grandfather sitting in a house beside a field, admonished to make sure his daughter never loses her faith. Even Bryan himself experienced the deception and role-playing of his malevolent visitors, who posed as his family, friends, and loved ones.

If I'm right here, then many NDErs have indeed been deceived into believing something that isn't true. If you're an NDE survivor yourself, I certainly don't want to invalidate your own anecdotal experience, but I believe there is a reason behind the deception, and it helps us better understand why we might experience what we do. So I'd like to offer my own explanation for this deception.

On one level, it may be a relief to hear that the reality of the afterlife may not be exactly as described in the DNDEs highlighted previously. For example, I have come to believe that in cases where NDErs report seeing children being torn apart by demons, or their friends being crucified upside down and burned alive, or helpless victims stuck in a vast sea of blood or viscous mud, these were merely manifestations introduced by the devious visitors and did not actually happen to "real" people. They were a virtual reality sold to the NDEr as real, but like the 150-foot flames that didn't burn the woman, they were merely an artificial apparition planted in the mind by those devious spiritual beings to terrify the NDEr.

But on another level, I've read some NDEs where the NDErs believed they were having a pleasant conversation with their father on a beautiful beach with a colorful sky overhead. And to hear that such a beautiful experience might actually have been a deceptively manifested reality within the confines of a small cubic cell can be challenging and distressing. Again, I don't want to invalidate anyone's anecdotal experience, but I also don't want anyone to go through life expecting the same beautiful experience at their final death, only to be rudely awakened to a much darker and more painful reality.

So why the deception? I believe it is purely a tactic of what the Christian worldview calls "spiritual warfare." So first I'd like to give you a little background on what exactly that means.

If you've made it this far in the book, I hope you've reached a point where you accept the existence of a spiritual reality beyond our material world. And as I've said, the Bible seems to clearly indicate that God has created other beings in the spiritual realm in addition to His creative efforts in our own material universe. And as with humanity, some of these spiritual beings have also rebelled against God.

As I pointed out earlier, Michael Heiser, in his book *The Unseen Realm*, makes a strong exegetical case for the fact that God has delegated authority over the human nations and kingdoms of this world to these other spiritual beings called the "sons of God," a belief derived primarily from Deuteronomy 32:8. Although the Masoretic text, the oldest copy of which dates from the 11th century AD, says that God "set boundaries for the nations according to the number of the *sons of Israel*", both the Septuagint and manuscripts discovered among the Dead Sea Scrolls, which predate the Masoretic text by more than 1,000 years, clearly end verse 8 with the phrase "sons of God." Heiser is one of a growing number of scholars who believe that Christians changed this phrase in later manuscript copies because it sounded too polytheistic or would diminish the divinity of Jesus as the one and only Son of God. Again, read his book if you want a more thorough analysis of this framework. The point is that Deuteronomy 32 seems to indicate that God delegated dominion over earthly kingdoms to these "sons of God," at times also called His "divine council," probably after the events of Babel in Genesis 11.

But what I want to highlight actually comes from Psalm 82:1, which says, "God presides in the great assembly; he judges among the gods." God later refers to these "gods" as the "sons of the Most High" (v6), confirming for us that these are the same "sons of God" referred to in Deuteronomy 32. According to this passage, God is passing judgment on these sons of God. And what is His judgment?

> How long will you defend the unjust and show partiality to the wicked? Defend the weak and the fatherless; uphold the cause of the poor and the oppressed. Rescue the weak and the needy; deliver them from the hand of the wicked.
> (Psalm 82:2-4 NLT)

God clearly calls out these sons of God for their actions that have caused evil and corruption in the kingdoms of men. They favor the wicked and the unjust. They leave the most vulnerable oppressed and without help. They forsake the powerless, abandoning them to the evil actions of the wicked. While it's certainly interesting to see that the blame for such evil and injustice in our world actually falls on these delegated rulers known as the sons of God, the more important point here is that these sons of God are in charge of the kingdoms of our world. They are the driving force behind the nations and the constant power struggle between them. So when we come into this world, we are actually born into their kingdoms, under their dominion, subject to their own rules and decisions, even if their will remains subject to God's ultimate authority. That's why Satan, the chief adversary of God, the leader of all those who oppose God's kingdom, is described by Jesus as the "ruler of this world" (John 12:31).

But that's exactly why the kingdom of God is a threat to them. God began his kingdom with a covenant promise through Abraham, culminating in the death and resurrection of Jesus. And now the "good news" that God's kingdom has come can spread throughout the world. That's why Jesus was so popular with the weak, the needy, and the powerless. They are the ones abandoned and underprivileged in the kingdoms of this world, they are the ones forsaken by the sons of God. And yet Jesus came not only to offer them a chance to be included in His kingdom, but to serve them and empower them to serve others in a similar way. God didn't expand His kingdom through bloodshed and power struggles, as the sons of God did, but rather through sacrificial love and humble elevation of others before Himself.

Thus, the kingdom of God is in direct conflict with other kingdoms ruled by the sons of God. Every time a person hears the good news that God's kingdom has come and decides to give his allegiance to Jesus as his Lord and King, he forsakes and abandons the ruler under whose dominion he was born. They become a turncoat, a traitor, a deserter. And this is a direct affront to the pride and arrogance of the rebellious spiritual beings who wanted to be their own god, to live by their own definitions of good and evil, and to rule their own kingdoms in the human world. So they will stop at nothing to prevent the loss of their kingdom subjects. Not because they care about us, but simply because, like rebellious men, they want more: more power, more authority, more dominion.

And this is essentially the background of the spiritual war into which we are born. We are merely pawns of our inherited spiritual rulers, born into kingdoms ruled by unrighteous spiritual beings to whom God has delegated authority. But God has seen the injustice they have sown, He has heard the cries of the weak and oppressed, and He is now moving through the hearts and minds of His followers to change the world, to invite as many people as possible to abandon the evil kingdoms they were born into and inherit a kingdom of justice, love and beauty. And our worldly spiritual rulers cannot allow this to happen.

> For we do not wrestle against flesh and blood, but against the rulers, against the authorities, against the cosmic powers over this present darkness, against

the spiritual forces of evil in the heavenly places.
(Ephesians 6:12 ESV)

Here in life, spiritual warfare can take many forms. It may be thoughts or ideas that are put into your mind. It can be sickness or disease. However, it can also be success, fame, and fortune. The purpose of spiritual warfare is not simply to make your life challenging, but rather to keep you from renouncing your present kingdom in favor of the kingdom of God.

Think of it this way. You were born into a prison cell that you cannot feel in any way; a prison cell under the authority of these unrighteous spiritual beings; a prison cell with the door wide open. The freedom of God's kingdom is just outside your door. As long as you remain quiet in the prison cell, you may be left alone because you're exactly where these spiritual forces want you to be. If you make a move toward the door, they will take whatever action is necessary to keep you in the cell. Maybe it's making you afraid of what's beyond the door, maybe it's making you loathe what's beyond the door, or love what's in the cell, or maybe it's something that actually physically prevents you from walking through the door. Whatever it takes, they will do it as long as you stay in the cell. They don't care that once you die, that prison cell closes forever with no hope of ever escaping. Their only goal is to keep you in that cell during your lifetime, subject to their own kingdom authority.

So how does this relate to deception in NDEs? If you're thinking critically, you probably already see the connection. These malevolent spiritual beings in Sheol were, and still are, members of the same spiritual kingdoms. They are under the rule of their own spiritual leaders, who have the same goal of preventing you from leaving their kingdoms for the kingdom of God.

But if you read enough NDE stories, you will find that it is often the most nightmarish, hellish NDEs that serve as a catalyst for conversion to Christianity. Understandably, when people experience such a horrific afterlife, they are much more likely to make changes in their lives to ensure that they don't meet the same fate at their final death. Conversely, those who have a pleasant or enjoyable NDE experience are not so inclined to make drastic changes in their lives or worldviews because they look forward to returning to that experience after death. So how might we apply this to the devious beings who reside in Sheol?

After observing human existence for thousands of years, these spiritual beings would surely be aware that sometimes people die, have a near-death experience, and then come back to life. So when a new human arrives in a cell, it might actually be better for them to keep a low profile for a while so as not to show their hand too soon. After all, if they immediately unleash the full measure of hellish torture only to have that human return to life, the experience may be a catalyst for losing that subject upon conversion to the kingdom of God. So we should expect that some DNDEs may not include a visit from these spiritual beings at all, which is certainly the case many times over.

But they also have other ways of ensuring that you don't feel the need to leave through that metaphorical prison door. For example, they may reaffirm your current worldview and try to reassure you that you are on the "right path." Like the man who met his father and grandfather and was admonished to make sure his daughter didn't lose her religion. This man would return from his NDE convinced that his Muslim faith would take him to Paradise after death, alongside his father and grandfather before him. And if I'm right about this particular example, the spiritual beings who deceptively played the role of his father and grandfather were trying to work through the NDEr to keep both him *and* his young daughter in their own metaphorical prison cells.

Or perhaps the spiritual beings may choose instead to sow a seed of confusion. They may pose as the Being of light, attempting to shower you with enchanting love and convince you that you actually had a pleasant NDE. They may pose as a close family member, offering words of comfort and reassurance that you're on the right path to Paradise after this life. Perhaps they would manifest as a religious figure from another religion, such as Buddha or Zeus, in an attempt to push you toward one of those other worldly religions. Maybe they would appear as a little blue fairy and feed you all sorts of lies about the universe, about life and death, or show you what they claim will be your next "reincarnated" life form. Or maybe they would even impersonate Jesus, but order you to crawl on the ground and kiss their disgusting, cracked, yellow toes.

I hope you are getting the big picture here. The point is that deception is only one of many tools used by the spiritual forces that rule our present world and reside in Sheol. They are motivated by their own selfish pride to keep you under their control and prevent you from leaving them in favor of God as your Lord and King. And whether in this life or during an NDE, if they have the opportunity, they will feed you anything that will keep you as their own subject. Not because they care about you, but because they simply don't want to relinquish their dominion over you.

In this light, the deception in NDEs that occur in the realm of Sheol makes perfect sense. It is merely a visible extension of the lies and deception we are fed every day in our constant struggle with the ongoing spiritual warfare into which we were born. It is my hope that readers of this book will gain clarity through this understanding, and that NDE survivors who have been subjected to such deception will have their eyes opened to better understand their experience and what it might mean for the rest of their lives here.

~ WHY TRUST BRYAN MELVIN ~

Since DNDEs seem to contain numerous instances of deception, and since I have previously warned against drawing conclusions about the afterlife from a single, anecdotal NDE, I am sure some will object to the fact that most of the entire framework is based on Bryan Melvin's near-death experience. Then why do I feel confident enough to spend countless hours over the past few years writing a book detailing this framework and exposing myself to the ridicule and judgment of others? What if Bryan's story was just another form of deception? The answer is that I believe Bryan's NDE is unique, and here is why.

Bryan began his journey with the textbook signs of a pleasant NDE: ascending to meet the Being of light, whom he specifically identifies as Jesus, in accordance with my beliefs as discussed in this book. And as I have stated in this chapter, I believe that Jesus has absolute power and authority over our lives and deaths, and in selecting a unique NDE to offer some of us at the time of our death. While some NDErs have been given elements of both a distressing and pleasant NDE, Bryan is unique here in that Jesus specifically *tells* Bryan that He is sending him on a journey to see something that needs to be seen. And then He puts Bryan into a swirling vortex that carries him to Sheol to begin his DNDE.

Unlike typical DNDErs, Bryan could not be harmed by the malevolent, demonic creatures that accompanied him in his cell, though certainly not for lack of trying. As sovereign Lord even over the realm of Sheol, the commands of Jesus could not be ignored by these malevolent spiritual beings, forcing them to obey His order to escort Bryan out of his cell and into the realm beyond the veil. Furthermore, when Jesus rescued Bryan from Sheol, He did so in the region outside of a cell, then carried him back into his cell, back through the vortex, and back into the realm of spiritual freedom where the entire journey had begun.

The conclusion must therefore be that Jesus was in charge of the entire experience, that Jesus wanted Bryan to see the world of Sheol beyond the walls of his cell, and that Jesus then brought Bryan back so that he could share this information with the rest of us in the land of the living. And since Bryan clearly began and ended his NDE in the realm of spiritual freedom with Jesus, we can trust that the experience itself was not simply another instance of deception. He certainly experienced deception while in his cell, but everything outside the cell was nothing but pure, unfiltered truth, a grim preview of the state of existence of billions of human souls in the spiritual confinement of Sheol.

~ WHY THIS BOOK ~

Wow! This has been an incredibly verbose chapter; I hope you were able to get through it without your eyes glazing over and your head nodding off to sleep. I'm not so much trying to give you the final answer to all these questions as I am trying to share my heart and help you understand what I believe and why I believe it. With that in mind, I'd like to respond to one last question: Why did I write this book? What is my purpose? What is my intention?

If I had to sum up my answer in a single sentence, it would be this: I wrote this book because I hope that all people will find their way to spiritual freedom and the renewed creation. But here is the long version.

I am a Christian, a term that literally means "a follower of Christ." As one who follows Jesus and all of His teachings, I am compelled to believe that Hell is a real place and that many beings will reside there (Matthew 25:41) and that it will be a place of torment for its inhabitants (Matthew 22:13). Although it is obvious, given my natural inclination toward selfishness and self-gratification, I am compelled to believe that I am utterly incapable of living according to the laws of God's kingdom (Romans 3:23), that I am a prisoner living in exile in the kingdoms of this world, which are built on wickedness and evil, and that because, left to my own devices, I would only serve to perpetuate and increase evil wherever I live, bringing pain and suffering to those around me, I must go to that prison called Hell when my life on Earth is complete (Romans 6:23).

Conversely, I am compelled to believe that God exists, that He resides in a spiritual kingdom called "Heaven" beyond our present material perception, and that Jesus is there waiting for His final day of revelation to the world (Mark 16:19). Furthermore, I am compelled to believe that when a member of God's kingdom dies, they are taken to be with Jesus in this heavenly paradise (Luke 23:43), and that they will all wait together in this place of rest for the final day of the Lord (John 5:29).

However, my religious upbringing didn't really prepare me for a concrete picture of what these two dichotomous existences might actually look like. I had a good understanding of the philosophy of Heaven and Hell, but no information about their ontology. As I'm sure was the case for many of you, my mind immediately went to the abstract concepts of white robes and harps sitting in the clouds, or red devils with pitchforks in fiery caves. But that all changed when I began to study near-death experiences.

For me, those truly pleasant NDEs, those NDEs basking in the beauty and warmth of the Being of light, inundated by the tenderness of deceased loved ones, overwhelmed by the unconditional love emanating from the Creator of the universe, those gave me an immense clarity of perspective on what existence in God's heavenly kingdom might be like. They taught me to see the emotional intimacy of it all, the deep connection with everyone else in that paradise, the fellowship and love they shared, the complete transparency that comes from knowing the thoughts and intentions of everyone around you. It was so much more beautiful than harps and clouds.

Likewise, the various types of distressing NDEs framed in my mind concrete images of what a life of torment in the outer darkness of Hell might be like. Whether it's the grief and isolation of the void, the torment of the pain and suffering we've caused others in life, or the terrifying instances of demonic torture, these NDEs revealed to me many aspects of what an existence in the spiritual confinement of Hell might be like. They, in turn, taught me to look beyond the superficial Biblical verbiage about Hell and begin to see the deeper context of how such a place might fit into the metanarrative of the Bible.

But more than anything, the intense emotional trauma described by DNDE survivors has played on my own empathetic responses, creating an indescribable sense of dread in me when I hear of someone's death. It's a sinking feeling, deep in my gut, but reaching all the way up to the back of my throat. An anxious tension, wondering if that person has descended through a swirling vortex or black tunnel into their own cell in Sheol, and now sits in the torment of their own isolation and grief, or even worse, has found themselves the unfortunate victim of immeasurably painful torture at the hands of foul, evil, devious creatures. The thought is unbearable.

From my own flawed perspective, I believe that much of our world has become blinded to our exile in these worldly kingdoms, blinded to the reality of Heaven and Hell, and blinded to the idea that our choices in this life have any real consequences. I think we have come to view worldviews (religious or otherwise) like cookies - we try a few, find one that suits our tastes, and just sort of settle into the norms of our choice. Taken to its logical conclusion, such a perspective on worldviews gives us a natural apprehension about trying to "convert" people from one worldview to another. Why can't you just let me enjoy my Snickerdoodle? Go eat your oatmeal raisin cookie and leave me alone! You do you, let me do me!

But if Heaven and Hell do exist, and if our membership in a particular kingdom, our adherence to a particular worldview, dictates whether we experience the afterlife in a state of blissful freedom or agonizing confinement, then things change a bit. The Christian worldview is no longer just another flavor of cookie to be selected based solely on individual taste, but rather the cure for the most significant problem plaguing humanity.

As a Christian, it's challenging because I know that God has given us the freedom to choose our kingdom allegiance. To choose to continue living in the worldly kingdoms we were born into, which leads down a path to a prison called Hell. Or to choose to turn coat and become a member of God's kingdom, which leads to rehabilitation and an eventual home with God when He unites the spiritual with the material. But at the same time, I am compelled to believe that those who choose the former will experience an afterlife consistent with the DNDE stories we discussed earlier in this book. And it's not like I can just choose not to believe it; it's a truth claim made by Jesus himself, the one I'm called to follow into God's kingdom. It's table stakes; non-negotiable. I had to do something to help more people see the importance of this decision, right here, right now. So I set out to write this book.

For the Christian, I set out to write a book that could educate on the true Biblical teachings about the intermediate state right after death, that would reframe our concepts of

Heaven and Hell, that would help us see the Biblical narrative through the themes of kingdoms and prisons. I set out to uncover the common threads within NDEs and offer an explanation for the oddities that typically scare most Christians away from the subject. I set out to strengthen the faith of Christians through the evidence from NDEs and to equip Christians to make a similar case to others and have an eternal impact on God's kingdom.

For the non-Christian, I set out to write a book that could help you see beyond the materialistic scientism that dominates our public discourse. In my opinion, NDEs offer compelling evidence for some kind of life after death, a life that offers a potential dichotomy between peace and torment, but with no immediately apparent connection to the divisive topic of "religion." NDEs are contemporaneous phenomena that happen every day to a large number of people, perhaps even people you know. They don't rely on deep philosophical arguments or an appeal to ancient religious texts to build a case for life after death, which makes them relatable to a larger audience of truth-seekers in today's society, even if they are not already religious. I framed this book the way I did because I hoped to build a cumulative case for the existence of an afterlife without religious baggage, so that you could allow yourself to follow the evidence where it really leads before triggering the emotional defenses that typically accompany discussions of worldviews. I truly believe that there are many out there who will find the evidence from NDEs to be a compelling reason to believe in an afterlife, and more specifically, to begin to view the world through the lens of Christianity. And if just one person decides to join God's kingdom after reading this book, then it will all have been worth it.

But being a part of God's kingdom isn't just about finding an afterlife of peace rather than torment. It's about living up to the purpose for which we were created, loving others, and creating more order and beauty in our world for the benefit of all life on this planet. As citizens in God's kingdom, we are active participants in God's rehabilitation plan which replaces our prison sentence in Hell. And along the way of this rehabilitation plan, we have the opportunity to create small pockets of God's kingdom in our present world that reflect, in a smaller way, what our world will look like at that future time when God brings His kingdom here on Earth as it is now in Heaven.

We saw this in the case of John Newton, the former slave trader who became a Christian and then became a leading abolitionist. He put his story into words when he wrote the gospel hymn Amazing Grace, telling how God's grace opened his eyes to his own tendencies toward the evils of racism, and it was God who saved him from his hateful, wretched state.

We saw this in the story of Ken Parker, a former Grand Dragon of the KKK who became a Christian, allowed God's Spirit to energize him, change his heart, and begin to rehabilitate him. Thanks to the work of God in him, he would later come out to publicly denounce the KKK and all other racist organizations.[79]

We saw this in the heroic actions of the Reverend Martin Luther King Jr. and Harriet Tubman, both of whom drew on the convictions of their Christian worldview to not only see the

---

[79] https://www.nbcnews.com/news/us-news/ex-kkk-member-denounces-hate-gro ups-one-year-after-rallying-n899326

injustice of their present age, but to courageously stand against it and impact our world for the better.

It is my hope that readers of this book will not only find spiritual freedom in the next life, but also embrace the purpose for which we were created and change our world for the better.

8

THE CHOICE

This book has undoubtedly been one of the most challenging and time-consuming endeavors I have undertaken in my entire life. Over the past few years, I have written, rewritten, and practically gutted entire sections of my manuscript in an effort to adequately illuminate for you the clear dichotomy revealed through NDEs, and to help you break down any emotional barrier that might ultimately consign you to Sheol when your life here is over. But, as Morpheus told Neo in The Matrix, I can only show you the way. It's up to you to choose which pill to swallow.

I've given you the evidence, I've given you what I believe to be a cogent explanation of that evidence, and I've pointed out the logical conclusions that must follow from that explanation. But I know that the battle may still be raging in your heart, in your mind, and in your spirit. I understand that.

You see, according to my worldview, I fully expect you to be bombarded by an onslaught of spiritual warfare tactics every time you try to read this book. Have you noticed times when you weren't motivated to read, or when you thought about just dropping the book? Did you notice instances of unexpected interruptions that kept you from progressing or focusing on the content of the book? Or maybe it came in the form of thoughts and ideas that dismissed the concepts of this book as Christian propaganda or nonsense? Migraines? Sickness? Did you just struggle to stay awake as you read it in bed? Okay, maybe I'm partly to blame for that last one; I am an engineer, after all, and we're not exactly known for our engaging conversation.

The point I'm trying to make is that I believe this book has the potential to help people escape that metaphorical prison cell, to renounce the kingdoms of this world in favor of the kingdom of God. And I know that such a movement will not be allowed to proceed without resistance. I can only hope that you will be given eyes to see what is really going on, because once you begin to see the outworking of spiritual warfare for what it really is, it becomes almost impossible to mistake it for anything else. And it is my hope that when you see this, when you feel the influence of these malevolent spiritual forces trying to keep you from leaving that prison cell, that you will see it as even more evidence and proof of the reality of what I'm presenting. They wouldn't attack you unless what you were moving towards was actually a credible and very real threat to their agenda.

So in the end, it all comes down to one simple question: who are you going to listen to?

The voices, much like the outcome that will result from your decision, could not be more different. To demonstrate this, I would like to end this book with one final near-death experience. I have chosen this NDE because I believe it not only perfectly summarizes the dichotomy between spiritual freedom and spiritual confinement, but also because it highlights the tone of voice and vocabulary reflected in each realm. I'll share some final thoughts on this particular NDE next, but first let's just read it together.

~ A Tale of Two Worlds ~

It was April 2006 and I was driving home from an event at my school going about 140 kmh in my car when I lost control. The car skidded sideways on the road, into the ditch, and then into a telephone pole. As soon as I struck the pole I remember total darkness. At this time in reality, the car had struck the pole sideways and my body was mangled and near-death inside the vehicle. I was transported to a hospital eighty miles away and was clinically dead for ten minutes. Okay - back to my point of view.

As soon as my car struck the pole, I saw nothing. Immediately, I presumed that I was dead, but soon realized that I was still conscious and this shouldn't be. I couldn't see, I couldn't smell, I couldn't feel anything and it was as if I was paralyzed but standing up at the same time. About this time, I started thinking to myself (not aloud) that this sucked and that I was right - I knew all along there would end up being no God or afterlife and that religion was nonsense. At the very moment that I thought this, the most terrifying experience of my life began.

Quietly at first, I began hearing non-worldly voices and screams of evil or laughter. I became scared and didn't know what was going on. The voices got louder and louder and soon, I could 'feel' the presence of beings or evil all around me. The voices began to become more distinctive and some of the 'beings' were shouting 'Come with us, come with us!! Haha, haha, heehee, Are you ready for it?!' in very scary voice tones. I began to realize that it sounded as though these were demons or evil beings associated with Satan. Even though before the experience I was very critical of religion and God, these things were convincing me otherwise and I immediately began saying 'Jesus loves me!!! The power of God will kill you all, Jesus save me!!' The beings started to yell, furious, 'There is no f****** God you pathetic ugly bastard! If there was a God your life would have been worth a sh**!!' And so I continued, 'Jesus save me!! I believe in you Jesus, God help me!' And the demons continued to yell and curse at me but at the same time they were slowly retracting from me and their presence was minimizing.

At this moment a piercing white, beam of light the width of a pen shot down to us. The demons began screaming and moaning, as if they were melting and soon they disappeared. The light was literally blinding but I could stare directly into it without flinching. I felt as though - I all of a sudden knew everything there was to know about everything and I felt this enormous presence of love and respect and everything good. Artistic portrayals of Jesus began flashing before my eyes, all different kinds of pictures and paintings and I saw a sequence of the crucifixion of Christ. The light was getting brighter at this time, and wider. Soon Jesus appeared in front of me and I could do nothing but fall to my knees and then lay my head on the floor at his feet. It was like that for an eternity and then Jesus said, 'You are worthy, child; rise.' So I did and faced the Lord Jesus Christ with utmost guilt and feelings of utter insignificance. Jesus said, 'You have learned from your mistakes my child. You will return, and you will show others the way. You will spread the love of God.' I immediately began to weep uncontrollably (yes even though I'm a seventeen year old dude) and kept saying, 'I am unworthy Lord.' At this moment, I was in the presence of my deceased relatives, two uncles, an aunt, a grandfather and a great-grandmother of whom none spoke but they pointed to the 'ground', indicating I must return. At this point, I was spontaneously in my mortal body in the hospital looking up at my parents and friends. They would never believe the story.[80]

~ My Interpretation ~

First, allow me to describe what I believe is happening here in light of the framework. Since the experience immediately cuts to black, I believe the young man was instantaneously transported to his cell in Sheol at the time of his death. His initial experience was that of the void reported in numerous other DNDEs. Note that he is fully conscious and aware of his existence, has feelings about the present situation, and quickly expresses feelings of anger and disappointment. And the distressing nature of his experience is compounded when malevolent spiritual beings descend upon him, another feature reported in many other DNDEs. Everything about his experience is perfectly consistent with the many DNDEs we have discussed earlier in this book and an existence in the spiritual confinement of Sheol, complete with a visit from malevolent beings who wish to torture him for fun.

But the experience diverges when Jesus arrives on the scene. Frankly, it's unclear to me whether Jesus brought the man out of the cell to visit deceased relatives in spiritual freedom, whether He brought those deceased relatives with Him for the temporary

---

[80] https://www.nderf.org/Experiences/1jedraine_c_nde.html

visit, or whether He merely used the walls of the cubic cell to project an image of those deceased relatives who remained in the realm of spiritual freedom (like a live video feed). I'm inclined to believe that the man remained in the cell throughout the visit with Jesus and his relatives because of the instantaneous return to his body, unlike Bryan and others in spiritual freedom who move continuously through a space leading back to the body, but I suppose it's possible that wasn't the case.

This does raise the possibility that the Jesus character was a demonic creature in disguise, but I'm not convinced. First, because all the other demonic creatures fled in fear, similar to the description in Bryan's account when Jesus rescued him from the Land Best Forgotten. And second, because the character and teachings of the NDE are 100% consistent with the Jesus revealed in the Bible - a loving, gentle demeanor that affirms the importance of loving others and helping to spread the love of God in the world. I don't believe that one of these devious creatures would impersonate Jesus and teach a message consistent with what Jesus taught, resulting in this young man's conversion to Christianity after his experience. That would be contrary to their goal of keeping the man in the spiritual kingdom into which he was born. For these reasons, I believe that it was indeed Jesus, the true Being of light, who visited this man in Sheol, spoke a message of affirmation and love, and changed his life forever.

The young man does not report a return to his body, but rather a sudden awakening in his body at the end of his experience. This again leads me to believe that he remained in his cell in Sheol throughout the experience and simply returned to his body as quickly as he left it.

So, given my current understanding of the framework, this is how I interpret this particular NDE. Perhaps now would be a good time for you to revisit some of your favorite NDE sources and again explore how well the framework fits the experiences as described by the survivors. But that's probably not absolutely necessary at this point. If you've read this far into the book, I have to assume that you're either a Christian who doesn't need any additional convincing, or you're a non-Christian who has found the framework compelling and is now simply looking for the next steps as we complete our journey together.

At any rate, before we get into some final thoughts, let's spend a little more time unpacking this particular NDE to take note of what it reveals about the dichotomy of spiritual freedom and spiritual confinement.

~ On Belief ~

Like many NDE survivors, this young man was a self-described atheist or agnostic who thought all religions were nonsense (you can read more details and additional questions he answered about the experience and his personal beliefs at the link in the footnote). But did you identify the moment when he changed his mind? It was when he encountered the evil of the malevolent beings that surrounded him and ridiculed him.

This underscores exactly what I said earlier about deception in Sheol. Again and again, when these demonic creatures come directly at the DNDErs, it serves as a very strong catalyst for the belief in a hellish afterlife, and drives significant motivation in the survivor to make whatever life changes are necessary to avoid ending up there at their final death. This man is now a Christian, according to his answers on the cited web page. He has forsaken the worldly kingdom into which he was born for the kingdom of God. They have lost their dominion over him. And this is precisely why I believe so many DNDErs are instead deceived into a false sense of security, enchanted by the emotional manipulation of these cunning, crafty creatures.

This man now knows for certain that there is an afterlife. He knows that the state of that life could be "the most terrifying experience" of your life, or it could be one of "love and respect and everything good." Like the thousands of accounts compiled into the statistics in Chapter 2, this man returned from his NDE with a renewed focus on the priority of love, abandoning his materialistic, atheistic worldview in favor of one that could actually explain his experience. It is my sincere hope that readers of this book will eventually arrive at the same conclusion and destination as the young man in this NDE.

~ The Environment ~

Observe the environment throughout the experience. Immediately after his death, his surroundings are dark, silent, and lonely. There is nothing to see, nothing to smell. It is an environment completely devoid of light, completely devoid of life. He existed in a state of conscious awareness, yet complete and utter isolation. Notice also how quickly he was flooded with feelings of disappointment, disillusionment, and even anger.

Again, this description fits perfectly with the void-type DNDE discussed earlier in this book. It also fits perfectly with a cubic cell in Sheol, a place designed to be cut off from God and all of His creation, protected from His rules and regulations, a place of anger and sorrow - grief over the lack of connection with God and all other beings. Much like the isolated hexagonal chambers to be launched into space in The Mitchells vs. the Machines, this is the true state of Hell as I have come to believe it. And I believe that, given enough time, the anger and grief this young man brought with him to the cell would have played out before his eyes in any number of scenes reminding him of the pain he had caused in his life, and reiterating the need to keep him locked up to protect the others he would only continue to hurt.

But we can contrast the darkness of Hell with the light of Jesus. The light was blinding and brilliant, yet he could look straight into it, as described by other NDErs. In the presence of the light emanating from Jesus, he found peace, knowledge, identity, and an "enormous presence of love and respect and everything good." He even had the opportunity to see and communicate with deceased loved ones.

This description is completely consistent with other NDE encounters with the Being of light - Jesus. It is just a taste of life after death in the spiritual freedom of Paradise. It shows us what an existence in the presence of God's heavenly kingdom might be like, together with our loved ones, resting in the beauty and splendor of the Light of the World (John 8:12).

This man now knows exactly what it feels like to exist in the spiritual confinement of Sheol as well as in the spiritual freedom of Paradise. He knows for certain that both exist, and that our choices in this life will determine our destination in the next. It is my sincere hope that all who read this book will find the start of their next life in the peace and love of spiritual freedom in Paradise.

~ THE LANGUAGE ~

Next, let's notice the words spoken by each group of spiritual beings. The demonic beings tear him down, tell him that his life is meaningless, mock his appearance, and call him pathetic. Their words are littered with trash and curses, steeped in hatred and disgust. Their only pleasure comes from the anticipation of the torture they will soon be able to inflict on this terrified young man.

This is entirely consistent with the patterns of speech revealed by a large sample of DNDEs. Many cited in this book contain clear instances of malicious, hurtful rhetoric hurled at survivors by these evil, devious beings, taunting them about painful personal issues and sowing seeds of fear within them.

But now look at Jesus. He calls this man His child, tells him he is worthy to stand before Him, and offers words of comfort, affirmation, and reassurance. His tone, words, and message abound with love, not only for the man himself, but for a broken world to which this man would bring that love.

This, too, is in alignment with the vast majority of NDEs, which consist of a message of grace and love. Like so many NDErs before him, this man has returned to life with a newfound emphasis on the importance of love, and an immense desire to share that love with a world so desperately in need of it.

This man now knows what it is to be bombarded by the malicious, evil, hurtful words found in the spiritual confinement of Sheol. Yet he also knows what it is to be overwhelmed by the gracious and compassionate words of Jesus, the very expression of love (1 John 4:8,16), in the realm of spiritual freedom. It is my sincere hope that all readers of this book will experience an afterlife filled with words of love and fellowship in the peaceful rest that is God's heavenly Paradise.

~ THE PURPOSE ~

To the demonic creatures, the young man's purpose was merely to go along with them, to participate in their sick games of torture, to be an object of their own amusement at the expense of his own terror and pain. He was to be the object of their mockery, the butt of their wicked jokes, and the victim of any number of heinous acts they could devise in their malevolent minds.

In continuity with previous discussion points, this is exactly in line with other DNDEs where the NDEr has been yelled at, put down, mocked, verbally taunted, and physically assaulted. Clearly, these foul beings who dwell in Sheol have nothing but evil within them.

In contrast, Jesus' purpose for the man was simply to tell others of the love he experienced while standing in the presence of the God of the universe. It was to love and be loved, the very purpose for which he was created.

This man has seen firsthand the distinct dichotomy between his purpose both in Sheol, among the assembly of the dead, and in Paradise, within the kingdom and family of God. This dichotomy highlights for us the difference between living a life for a subjective purpose, in which we are valued only by what we can offer others in the present moment, and a transcendent purpose, in which we exist to participate in the outpouring of an eternal love shared within the divine community of God, to receive God's love and reflect that love back to all others around us, and to be adopted into the family of God forever.

I don't know about you, but I long for the latter purpose in that statement. I long to be part of a family, to be part of a community of love and respect, to love and be loved. I doubt I'm alone in this sentiment, because there are so many instances in movies where we practically idolize this ideal of community and fellowship. I'm sure you can think of countless examples, but here's one that comes to mind.

The 1988 film "Twins" stars Arnold Schwarzenegger and Danny DeVito as an unlikely pair of twin brothers. Although there are several story arcs that tie the entire film together, one of the primary arcs is their joint quest to find their birth mother, with whom they have had no relationship for their entire lives. Schwarzenegger grew up on an idyllic island paradise, where he was loved and given a classical education, while DeVito grew up as an orphan, in and out of foster homes and juvenile detention centers throughout his life.

~ Spoiler Alert ~

Their search eventually leads them to the office of the scientist who conducted the experiment that led to their birth, and finally provides context for the disparity between the main characters. The experiment involved taking genetic material from half a dozen men who epitomized physical, mental, and emotional achievement and combining it with the genetic material of an ideal woman in an effort to create the most evolved, sophisticated human being in existence.

But when the embryo split into twins, it didn't split evenly. According to the lead scientist, all that was good and pure went into Schwarzenegger, and all the rest of the junk went into DeVito. Understandably, this news is devastating to DeVito, who leaves the building with a noticeable slump in his gait and a deep depression in his spirit.

~ End of Spoilers ~

In this particular moment of depression and sadness, Schwarzenegger manages to lift DeVito's spirits by mentioning one thing: family. "You're the missing part of my life. And I'm the missing part of your life. And when we find mama, we can fill the missing part of hers. We won't be alone anymore. We can be a family," he says. As the light returns to DeVito's eyes, they share messages of hope about the beautiful things we so often associate with a loving family: a Christmas tree, Thanksgiving dinner, and a real home where you're always welcome, even when you've been bad.

The tender embrace shared by the two protagonists in this moment is a perfect embodiment of the hope we long for, a perfect representation of the comfort we find in this sense of belonging, in the community and fellowship of a family built on the central premise of unconditional love. And it is this longing, this ideal, that perfectly reflects our destiny in the family of the kingdom of God. And it is a hope with a promise of fulfillment.

We have the opportunity for guaranteed access to this community of unconditional love. But it is up to us to make that choice.

~ CHOOSE A SIDE ~

The man in the NDE above was fortunate. As an avowed atheist/agnostic whose nature had not been rehabilitated, his final destination after death would have been that cell in Sheol. He would have spent the beginning of his next life in that dark, lonely void, where for a time he would have found company only with those evil, demonic creatures who would undoubtedly have subjected him to countless forms of torture while they had the opportunity. Yet he was given a gift - a glimpse of what the future might be like, and a visit from the God of the universe, overwhelmed by love and comfort. And he was sent back for a second chance. A chance to tell his story, a chance to share that amazing love, and a chance to make sure that he took God's path of rehabilitation and accepted the invitation to join God's kingdom before his final death.

But not all of us will be so fortunate. For most of us, our first death marks the beginning of our second life, our eternal spiritual life. And the state of that life will either be one of confinement, darkness, loneliness, anger, and grief. Or it will be one of freedom, comfort, love, light, companionship, and fellowship. That state will be determined solely by the choice we make in this life, our choice of kingdom citizenship.

So what will it be? Will you follow the evidence from NDEs, from thousands of eyewitnesses to an all-loving, all-knowing, transcendent Being who has sovereignty and power over the life and death of every individual on this planet, from numerous accounts of both heavenly bliss and hellish torment, and come to accept the existence of life after death and the truth of the Christian worldview? And if so, will you choose to submit to God's definition of good and evil and live to your full potential as a human image of God in this life, or will you create your own definition of good and evil and ensure that our world remains as broken as it is today? You may not like it, you may not agree with it, it may not be how you would have done things if you were in charge, but if it's true, are you willing to follow your feelings right into that inevitable cell in Sheol? I can't make that decision for you; I can only warn you of the consequences, based on everything we've covered in this book. Just as Adam and Eve had a choice between two trees, we all face a similar choice in how we will live.

You could choose to live life as you see fit, to live your own truth, to trust your own understanding of the world, to be your best self, to pursue the idols of power, money, sex, pride, fame, or any other glittering distraction that will mean nothing after death. You could embrace and celebrate your worldly desires, rationalize them, wave them away as "born that way." But in the end, this path will most likely lead you to that prison called Hell, where you will remain in isolation because, at some point in the eternal future, you would cause harm or pain when these things are no longer tolerated. Your unrehabilitated nature would corrupt the renewed heavens and earth, so you will be cut off from this restored creation and allowed to live in your own little world, living by your own rules, with your own definitions of good and evil.

Alternatively, you could choose to live your life by and for God, walking with Him and striving to know and imitate Him more, allowing yourself to be His servant here on Earth, loving others as He loves them, regardless of race, religion or ethnicity. You could allow God to change you and make you more like Him, giving you the willpower over time to break free from your desires for the things of this world. You could allow yourself to be rehabilitated, changed from the inside out, so that you will be prepared to live in God's kingdom, at peace with all other life, in a renewed and perfected material utopian universe, forever. This choice means accepting God's freely offered gift of eternal life with Him rather than in the prison called Hell, recognizing that it is given because of His grace, in accordance with His justice, and regardless of your actions or merits. It means trusting Jesus' death as a sufficient sacrifice to cover all your imperfections, and trusting God the Father to keep His promise of grace and mercy and bring you to be with Him in perfect fellowship for all eternity. It means consciously choosing to walk away from what you thought it meant to be human and seeking to live in God's kingdom, submitting to His rules and trusting Him to succeed in you where you have failed.

So what will you choose? NDEs give us everything we need to be absolutely certain of life after death, and the Bible gives us everything we need to be absolutely certain of what life we will find at that time. Are you ready to choose a side? Are you sure of the life you will inherit after this one? Will you wake up to an eternal prison cell or to an eternal fellowship with your Creator and Lover of your soul? The choice is yours. The time is now.

If you've found the case presented in this book compelling, and you're not already a Christian, I want to offer to help you take the first step toward citizenship in God's kingdom. This is not a magic spell; the words themselves mean nothing. It's the expression of your heart and the conviction of your resolve that give meaning. Thank you for taking the time to explore what I've outlined in this book. I hope it has made a difference in your life, both here and now, and in the afterlife to come.

God, thank you for opening my eyes to the truth of your kingdom. Thank you for protecting me from myself and spiritual forces of darkness so that I could set aside my own emotional objections and see the truth for what it really is. I know that I have not lived up to your definition of good and evil, that I am unfit to rule justly over Your creation, and that I have been living in a state of rebellion against you. But today, I am declaring to you that I want to live differently. I want to become a part of your kingdom, I want to experience first-hand the overflowing of your abundant love, and I want to become an active participant in making this world a better place. Forgive me for propagating pain and suffering in this world, and help me to know you more, help me to grow in imitation of your love, help me to see the world the way you see it. Today I turn from my previous life and I am dedicating my life to you and to the growth and advancement of your kingdom, both now, and into eternity. Thank you, Jesus, for showing me what that looks like through your life, and thank you for making it possible through your death. Teach me to know you, follow you, and love you as you love me. Amen.

God grants you life; will you now walk with God, decreasing ugliness in the land, as an extension of the Master's Hands? Or will you walk away from God ensuring ugliness remains where you trod? [81]

---

[81] Jesus. As cited by Bryan Melvin in *A Land Unknown: Hell's Dominion*